Faith, Hope and Chastity

Faith, Hope and Chastity

Honest Reflections from the Catholic Priesthood

Edited by Carolyn Butler

Fount
An Imprint of HarperCollins*Publishers*

Fount is an Imprint of
HarperCollins*Religious*
Part of HarperCollins*Publishers*
77–85 Fulham Palace Road, London W6 8JB

First published in Great Britain in 1999 by Fount

1 3 5 7 9 10 8 6 4 2

Carolyn Butler asserts the moral right to
be identified as the editor of this work

A catalogue record for this book
is available from the British Library

ISBN 0 00 628136 2

Printed and bound in Great Britain by
Creative Print and Design (Wales), Ebbw Vale

For my mother, Angela Lambert

Contents

Acknowledgements

I will never forget the day I sat down in my sitting room with my mother, a distinguished journalist and the author of eight successful books, and told her that I had decided to write a book. Excited but fearful, I awaited her reaction – not to the prospect of compiling a book, but to the idea of interviewing men from the priesthood. As a non-religious person with a ferocious and critical intellect, her response was crucial. To my great relief, it was also positive. As my mentor and guide, her editorial eye has played a large part in the production of this book – sometimes gentle, sometimes not so gentle, but always honest. It is to her and her unending support that I owe the greatest debt of thanks. Her wisdom has taught me a great deal.

Another big thank-you must go to Penelope Dunn, my agent at A. P. Watt, who has worked so hard on my behalf and with such excellent results. My husband Malcolm, and my children Luci, Sarah, Calum, Francis and Alexandra, are all in store for extra warm hugs and kisses, especially Malcolm who has taken the children away on strategic visits to relations for the occasional but critical 24 hours. Nobody told me that having a family would be such relentless hard work but also such riotous good fun. Their support has meant everything to me.

And finally, but absolutely crucially, I must thank the priests who contributed to this book. Roughly two thirds of the men whom I originally approached agreed to be interviewed – often after weeks of discussion and prayer. Their decisions were particularly courageous since in the Catholic Church we all to some extent feel the weight of the hierarchy – wherever it may be – bearing down on us. These priests' words will forever bear witness to their own noble and often painful ministries while illustrating the fine and honourable calibre of the priesthood today. To have glimpsed some of the deeper moments of their lives has been a privilege for which I am eternally grateful.

Carolyn Butler, London, November 1998

Introduction

Struggle and success are the themes of this book. What are the struggles faced by Catholic priests today, and, more importantly, how do they overcome them? We can usually understand why priests leave the ministry, but do we understand why they stay? The interviews which follow explore in detail the lives of 17 priests who have not only experienced controversy within their ministry – be it sexual or political – but have come through that conflict with a stronger and more integrated understanding of God and their vocation.

The ingredients which make up a successful ministry are hard to understand. In some ways a good ministry is like a good marriage: mysterious, unique and reluctant to be probed. The reasons for this are many, the most immediate of which is often a basic superstition to leave well alone. Modesty also plays a part: most people are reluctant to gloat. The result is that we hear little if anything about successful marriages, or, in this case, successful priests. Failure seems to make better copy.

My decision to become a Catholic is one of the factors which lies behind this book. I was 22 then and am 36 now so enough time has elapsed for me to think about that early step, together with its ever-unfolding implications. Why I did it and where it is leading me are the questions which drive this book; inevitably it has been a very private odyssey. Taking two years to compile and coinciding not only with the birth of my fifth child but with the production of a second and less personal book on Cardinal Basil Hume, this collection of interviews has left my questions in many ways unanswered. I still do not quite understand why I took that decision all those years ago to become a Catholic. Beyond the psychological and cultural reasons there is a gap – a missing piece of the puzzle which I continue to question and which I can only attribute to the hand of God. Like the person in the lottery advertisement, I feel I have been tapped on the shoulder and my instinctive response is, 'Why me?'

The work of faith – what I call the 'inside work' – is a hard and sometimes grim road down which to trudge. Many of the contributors talk about the struggles associated with a life of prayer and the dilemmas it throws up in the face of other, more worldly demands. Nevertheless, now that the book is complete, I am left with the overriding impression that it is this inner life which bears the real fruit – the truly life-changing and everlasting fruit. Having witnessed the work of the Spirit in many but not all of the contributors, I find it something virtually impossible to describe other than to say what it is not. It is not, for example, primarily intellectual, although of course a rich prayer life will no doubt lead to a heightening of mental creativity. It is not particularly emotional, although personal feelings may well be lighter with joy or deeper with sorrow. And it is not necessarily psychological, although a certain inner calm and sense of rootedness may well develop. At this point on my own rough and difficult path, the best word I can find is radiance. There is in some of the priests I have interviewed an inner radiance which throws its light far beyond the individual concerned. Faith is present. God is close.

To be near this holiness is to experience a tiny portion of the divine. For myself the immediate and practical effect of this has been a sense of inspiration; I personally have felt the urge to better myself, to renew my prayer life, to help my fellow human beings, to benefit mankind. The longer-lasting but more generalized memory is of goodness; clear, simple and true.

The priests themselves represent as wide a cross-section as possible from missionaries to seminarians and parish priests to bishops; aside from this, they were not chosen according to any particular criteria. Having worked for the Catholic Church I simply knew or had heard of many priests whose stories struck me as rare and thought-provoking examples of faith today.

The purpose of this book has been to seek God in others, to catch something of God for myself and to share that with readers. I know now that while I may never fully understand my own decision to convert, I can at least appreciate that with each passing year the roots of faith have descended ever more deeply into their soil – not always obvious but still very much there. And there are times when, in the solitude of mortality, it is the quest itself, searching for God, that seems to matter most. This book is part of that search.

Foreword

by Cardinal Basil Hume OSB

Much has been written, and I am sure is still to be written, about priesthood. It is a subject approached from many angles. Biblical studies might concentrate on priesthood in the Old Testament, priesthood in the early Church and the whole notion of Christ the High Priest in the letter to the Hebrews. Those more directly concerned with priestly formation might reflect on how candidates are formed for priestly ministry today and that in itself begs the question, 'Just what is the role of the priest?'

Some may be familiar with the humorous quotation about the priest which runs along the lines of, 'If the sermon is lengthy, he is long-winded; if it is too short, he is ill-prepared; if he is out visiting, he is too sociable; if he doesn't visit, he is tied to his desk.' It ends by saying, 'When he dies, there's been no one like him!' Such humour does raise the question about the role of the priest and many phrases spring to mind that are often used in an attempt to answer this question: empowerer of the laity, leader of the community, ordinary celebrant of the sacraments – of course the list could go on and on.

However, many of these responses try to look at the priest in terms of what he does. I believe, before any functions or roles are even mentioned, it is important to go back and ask first of all what a priest is.

To begin with there is a common priesthood of all believers. The Catechism of the Catholic Church starts its reflection on the sacrament of Holy Orders by defining the entire community of believers as 'priestly': 'The faithful exercise their baptismal priesthood through their participation, each according to his own vocation, in Christ's mission as priest, prophet and king. Through the sacraments of Baptism and Confirmation the faithful are "consecrated to be ... a holy priesthood" ' (CCC 1546).

The Catechism then goes on to highlight the difference between this baptismal priesthood and what it terms 'ministerial priesthood' which is at the service of the common priesthood. 'It is directed at the unfolding of the baptismal grace of all Christians. The ministerial priesthood is a means by which Christ unceasingly builds up and leads his Church. For this reason it is transmitted by its own sacrament, the sacrament of Holy Orders' (CCC 1547).

For myself there is the fact of being a monk as well as a priest. The reflection which follows looks at some aspects of this and was preached at Ampleforth on the ordination of six monks to the priesthood.

* * *

Most often priesthood is spoken of in terms of function and is justified as providing for the spiritual needs of others. The priest is concerned with proclaiming and explaining the Word of God, with administering the sacraments and pre-eminently with celebrating the Eucharist. The priest acts as Christ's instrument. Saying that we act 'in persona Christi' not only shows how noble a thing it is to be a priest, but also how very daunting. We are but earthenware vessels and yet we have been entrusted with great riches.

I would like to speak about an aspect of Christ's priesthood which is linked very closely to our monastic profession. I have in mind both that total self-offering of ourselves when we pronounce our monastic vows and that self-offering of Christ to his Father, which is the true meaning of his sacrifice. You recall the words he spoke from the Cross: 'Into your hands, Father, I commend my spirit', words which express obedience, trust, love and abandonment to the divine will. At our monastic profession we echo those words of Christ when we sing, 'Suscipe me, Domine ... receive me, Lord, in accordance with your word, and I shall live. Do not let me be disappointed in my expectation.'

Every baptized person identifies with Christ's offering of himself and shares with him in his offering as priest and victim. What, then, is special about the monk's self-offering? Monastic life, as you know well, is a radical way of living out our baptismal promises. From this point of view our self-offering as monks is no different to the self-offering of any of the baptized. But ordination to the priesthood unites us in a special manner to the priesthood of Christ. It changes the character of our self-offering. It is no longer just monastic, it is also priestly. The monk-priest is not just a phenomenon which has arisen in history because of pastoral needs; it is a specific vocation within the monastic charism. It is a particular way of being a monk.

Although a monk-priest's life will often be spent 'hidden with Christ in God' and with no pastoral involvement, nonetheless, he is always a priest in and for the Church. Just to be a priest, at one with Christ's self-offering, is a value in itself; priesthood needs no other justification. This, however, is not the situation for us, as monk-priests of the English Benedictine Congregation. We are involved in pastoral work, notably in our schools, our parishes and in our service to the many hundreds of guests who visit us and share our prayer – all of whom form that larger community that is the extended monastic family. For them we must be icons of Christ the High Priest, teaching, sanctifying, and shepherding, as well as true sons of St Benedict.

It is the function of a monk to seek God in community, to spend much time singing His praises and worshipping Him, to reflect on God's revelation of Himself and to become daily more like Christ, trusting, loving, abandoned to the will of His Father.

Soon we shall be joined by the saints in heaven, sharing with us the joy of the gift of six new priests to the Church and to the monastic community of Ampleforth.

All this enriches our priesthood.

1. Father Peter Haverty (Opus Dei)

Fr Peter Haverty was born at Kippax,
near Leeds in 1934

I wondered, as I sat on the train to Manchester, what Fr Peter Haverty would wear. While priestly attire varies from total 'mufti' to full clerical garb, the majority of priests opt for a comfortable compromise of black trousers, black cardigan and a dark open-necked shirt. I was in for a surprise. As the taxi driver pulled up outside the house, I became aware of a dark flapping presence. This, I realized, was Fr Haverty – in a black cassock and proceeding down the road to greet me.

On entering the house – dimly lit and sparsely furnished – Fr Haverty, one of the first Opus Dei priests ordained in this country, suggested I might like to keep my coat on. Surprised but indeed quite cold I was happy to do just that. Fr Haverty then took me to a little chapel upstairs where we briefly prayed before arranging ourselves in the sitting room – the door left appropriately open – and embarking on the interview. Almost immediately after starting the clock chimed midday and Fr Haverty stopped the conversation. It was time for the Angelus, the traditional Catholic prayer recited at midday. 'Would you prefer to say it in English?' he asked. 'Yes,' I answered, feeling every inch the convert.

Fr Haverty disturbed me. Being with him was like travelling back in time to the pre-conciliar Church of the fifties – the clerical garb, the Angelus, the formality – the assumed authority. It was what he said, however, that really surprised me. When charged with the view that Opus Dei encourages self-flagellation, or that it primarily seeks out the rich, Fr Haverty rose to the challenge. Far from squirming under pressure or blaming the media

for its unfair coverage of Opus Dei as an extreme right-wing sect,
he simply explained openly and proudly the teachings of the
Blessed Josemaria, the founder of Opus Dei and the man who
those within it call 'the Father'.

I came away in conflict. Much of what Fr Haverty had said
would be laughable to the punter in the street – especially the
numerous references to angels and various heavenly beings.
Other aspects, however, were impressive in their orthodoxy,
while his emphasis on prayer, spiritual readings, the daily exam-
ination of conscience and the Mass was authoritative. For many
people these are the nuts and bolts of Catholic faith which
constantly need tightening, and they appreciate not just the
reminder but the conviction of the messenger. There is a thin
line, however, between conviction and spiritual arrogance; the
side on which Fr Haverty finds himself is for readers to decide.

On the eleventh of August 1958 at eight o'clock in the evening
I met the founder of Opus Dei. That was a big moment in my life.
I didn't know Spanish but I was accompanied by a priest, Fr James
Planell, who did a running translation for me. Mgr Escriva, as he
then was – now of course he's the Blessed Josemaria – talked a lot
about apostolate, usually referred to nowadays as evangelization,
and how difficult it is in England because although the English
have a heart, they don't like to let you see it. The Blessed Josemaria said, 'We're just about to make St Thomas More an "inter-
cessor", or patron of Opus Dei. He was a layman, he was married,
he loved his family and wife, he was good at his job and he loved
God. You see, he had all the ingredients.'

That was a really wonderful occasion. Blessed Josemaria was so
affectionate and so loving; he had such a warm personality. If you
know anybody who has ever met the Father, as we call him in Opus
Dei, they will agree. At the end of our conversation he turned to
address Fr Planell and asked him whether I was the one being pro-
posed for study in Rome. Hearing the word 'Roma', even I, not
understanding Spanish, could work out what that meant, so when
we got into the car I said to Fr Planell, 'What's this about Rome?'

'Well,' he replied, 'we were going to ask you later. The thing is,
would you like to go to Rome to study for the priesthood?'

'Yes,' I said. 'Yes, if you like.' I think at the time I was just happy to do whatever God had decided. As far as my life was concerned He seemed to know far more about it than I did. God had taken over.

I first became involved with Opus Dei when I studied Chemical Engineering at Imperial College in London. My mother had gone to the Bishop of Leeds – Bishop Heenan, later Cardinal Archbishop of Westminster – who in those days had an open day every Friday when people could go along to see him. She asked whether there was anywhere her son could stay in London – a Catholic residence of some description. 'Well,' he said, 'as a matter of fact this leaflet has just arrived on my desk,' and it was Netherhall House – a university hall of residence in Hampstead, with accommodation at that time for about 40 students – now it can take 100. I went to Netherhall House in 1953, just a few days before the start of the autumn term. I was 18 at the time. I remember being very taken with the idea of going to Mass every morning, which I'd never done before. I also started chatting to a priest called Fr John Galarraga – a Basque name – who had been ordained just over a year before although he was already in his thirties. It was over the next two years that I got more and more interested in Opus Dei.

By the springtime of '54 I was thinking, 'This is marvellous; Opus Dei is a wonderful, wonderful idea.' I was moved by the atmosphere and the straightforwardness of the people. It didn't take very long before I realized which of the residents were members of Opus Dei. Those in Opus Dei were always so gracious, so very 'supernatural'. I'll give you an example of what I mean by supernatural. One day we were in the study room and one of the residents was criticizing a priest.

'Do you know what the latest thing is?' he exclaimed. 'He's got himself an electric mop!'

They all laughed and said, 'What does he need with an electric mop? Where's his spirit of poverty?' There was a member of Opus Dei there who was studying. I remember how he sat with his head in his hands poring over his book, and how he simply looked up and said, 'Do you not think we ought to pray for this good priest?' And then went back to his studies, just like that. This odd remark struck me very forcibly; it seemed so supernatural. He wasn't criticizing, he wasn't complaining or arguing. He simply said, 'Let's pray for him.'

When I finished at Imperial College I went off to work in an ordnance factory in Bridgwater, Somerset. It was a graduate apprenticeship which I applied for in order to avoid National Service. I remember Father John Galarraga saying to me, 'Nobody has ever lost their vocation through being in the army; Opus Dei is for everybody, for people in all walks of life.' But I'd seen a couple of lads on National Service while I was doing vacation work in Hartlepool and they were just wasting their time polishing ammunition. 'I'm not going to waste my time like that,' I thought.

So there I was in Bridgwater, a Supernumerary member of Opus Dei and single, although at that stage I was still free to marry. I used to go up to London every month and on one of these journeys Fr Galarraga asked me whether I would like to be an Associate member, which I knew entailed a commitment to the celibate life. I agreed and then a year later was asked if I would like to be a Numerary. Again I said yes, although again I didn't realize the full implication of this: that God would later call me to be a priest – the priest members of Opus Dei being drawn from the Numerary members as a rule. In practice, whether Supernumerary, Associate or Numerary it was really all the same to me. The basic idea was to get up early in the morning, pray, go to Mass, go to work, say the Angelus at twelve o'clock, do some spiritual reading, say the rosary – all three parts of it then – return from work, pray some more and then at the end of the day make a general examination of conscience. There wasn't much time to spare except occasionally to go to the pub, where I would chat to friends about God, or about Opus Dei: in other words I would 'do apostolate' as we would say.

Then in August of 1958 I got this letter asking me to hand in my resignation at the factory in order to return to London. I didn't understand then what this might lead to but having checked that I was still eligible for membership of the Institute of Mechanical Engineers, I got on my Bantam motorbike and drove up to London. Given that I did not fully grasp the reason for handing in my notice, and without having another job lined up, this could be seen as a 'heroic act for God' – one of the criteria necessary for canonization. I had in fact applied previously for a coal-washing

FAITH, HOPE AND CHASTITY

post in Burton-on-Trent – another job exempt from National Service – but I gave that up as well. To be candid, you could hardly call giving up washing coal, which involved getting rid of all the dust and impurities, a great sacrifice! The reason I left the Bridgwater factory early was because the Blessed Josemaria had arrived in London.

After my encounter with the Blessed Josemaria, and as soon as my papers were in order, I set off for Rome. Pope John XXIII was elected almost immediately after I arrived and I was privileged to receive his first blessing in St Peter's Square. But I must say I found the languages very hard. We spoke a lot of Italian and Spanish and the lectures were in Latin! I'd done O level Latin, but I had to work through the other two foreign languages before I could get to the Latin, which was the only one I actually knew quite well. I began to think I was some sort of idiot, especially when I saw all the other students making rapid progress. In the end I managed to get through the exams but I must say I found it hard. I'm intellectually proud and don't like to feel stupid; at the age of 23 it was much more of a struggle to absorb things!

Once ordained I went to Barcelona in Spain for a year which was a great experience. I had to give half-hour meditations in Spanish, and after my slow start in Rome with the languages I did quite well. But I wasn't very happy as a celebrant in solemn liturgical ceremonies; I got very nervous. For example in Barcelona there was a big residence for girls and on Good Friday it was my turn to be principal celebrant. One priest was holding the missal for me to read the music and another was uncovering the Cross ready for veneration; he accidentally tore the cloth which didn't help my composure at all. As a good priest you have to learn to do these ceremonies well and the Blessed Josemaria wanted us to do them well for love of Our Lord. I think my unease is to do with my background in engineering; most of the priests I've met are good singers and they revel in liturgical ceremonies. I found it difficult and used to think to myself, 'Thank goodness the ceremonies are over now.' And yet I should have said, 'Look at the way the Pope goes through these massive ceremonies without turning a hair. He gets up and just knows what to do in a very complicated ceremony.' This is why we have a Master of Ceremonies who comes along and touches one on the elbow saying,

'Come on, it's time to go over to the lectern now.' 'Oh,' I say. 'It's me again is it?' I'm always bewildered by the process.

The Blessed Josemaria used to say, 'Of a hundred souls we're interested in a hundred.' He was a clever man – exceptionally bright, I'd say. He realized that in order to reach all the people in the world, you've got to go to the ones who have the most influence first – the university professors and the people in the media – precisely so that through them you can reach persons of every walk of life. The man who sweeps the streets cannot immediately influence the people around him or the laws of society. Once Opus Dei is well-established in a country it will reach out to all and sundry because God is interested in each and every person.

If you go to South American countries – for instance Venezuela – they put the Blessed Josemaria's face on their stamps. Why have they done that? It's out of gratitude for his work and the apostolate of the agricultural schools which have been promoted by Opus Dei to help the country-people farm their land better and so on. In other words, it's because the Father has done so much for the poor in these countries. These projects are called 'corporate works' and the equivalent over here would be the university residences, but in agricultural countries they are adapted to the needs of the poor.

Opus Dei is interested in the Christianization of the whole of society, so we do have a great deal of interest in helping intellectuals to become Christian. We also teach everybody to sanctify their work – whatever it is – for when God created man he told him to give everything its name and he placed man in the garden to beautify it and sanctify it. It's through sanctifying our work and our activities that we help people to reach God and to love Him. The women of Opus Dei, for example, who are engaged in domestic work, make things very clean; they polish the furniture and the doorknobs so that they shine. Through their work they profess the love and the glory of God.

The progress of Opus Dei has a lot to do with the holiness of the Blessed Josemaria, just as our work with souls depends on prayer and mortification. The Blessed Josemaria used to do extraordinary penances which people today would find unusual. But if you've read the lives of the saints you would find exactly the same: St Francis of Assisi, for example, lived in a hole in the

FAITH, HOPE AND CHASTITY

ground; a follower of St Francis, St Peter of Alcantara, slept for only two or three hours a night and used a stone for a pillow; St John of the Cross and St Peter Damian did extraordinary penances too. In the early days of Opus Dei, when things were not going so well, Blessed Josemaria would ask, 'What am I to do?' and would invariably come up with the same conclusion. He would scourge himself with a terrible 'discipline', or whip, which drew blood. This happened during the Spanish Civil War when the Church was violently persecuted. Sacrileges were committed against the Blessed Sacrament, and about 6,000 priests and nuns were assassinated. Blessed Josemaria offered his voluntary penances as reparation for these sins. He never said we all had to do this, but he did ask those of us who are Numeraries to practise a certain measure of corporal mortification. It's not such a fierce thing and there's no question of blood being spilt or flagellation. One mortification we use is the cilice – from the Latin *cilicium* meaning sackcloth. It's a little chain we put round our leg and it's more of a nuisance than a physical pain. As many people know, Pope Paul VI used a cilice as part of his penance for the Church – perhaps when he saw so many priests and nuns abandoning their vocation.

It would be misleading to attach too much importance to mortification. The Blessed Josemaria said the most difficult mortifications are the little ones which we meet every day: putting up with the annoying habits of the people we live with or work with, trying to be punctual with our appointments, keeping quiet when someone else is talking and trying not to say something irrelevant, accepting the discomforts of the weather, the aches and pains of the body and the traffic lights which have a habit of turning red just as we're approaching. But then all the mortification in the world is worthless unless it's offered to God with love and purity of intention. The Blessed Josemaria's advice was to offer our little sacrifices for some supernatural – or spiritual – motive, for example for the holy souls in purgatory, or for a person who needs spiritual help in overcoming temptations or fears. The founder of Opus Dei used to say that in our prayers we should parade our friends before Our Lord in the tabernacle and tell Jesus how good and deserving they are of His blessings and His grace. But then of course when we pray for others in this way we may hear Our Lord whispering in our ear, 'What are you going to do to back up this prayer? Do you really mean it?' In the Gospel Jesus said that sin could only be cast out through prayer and fasting, and fasting amounts to mortification. So, accepting an inconsiderate remark such as, 'Isn't your hair greasy?' or, 'You are looking a little the worse for wear today – have you not been sleeping so well?' is sometimes harder because of pride than the acceptance of severe physical pain. Other mortifications are getting up on time in the morning – the 'heroic minute' – tidying our desk or drawers, washing up after other people have left the dishes in the sink and so on.

There's nothing like realizing that the love of God has touched a heart, there's nothing like it in the world – just knowing that when a person responds to the love of God, Our Lord is working through me as the priest and He is pleased that this soul is responding to Him. As a priest I share in that joy. I remember just before my ordination in 1962 we received a talk from Don Ricardo Fernandez, one of the first priests of Opus Dei. We said to him, 'What is the most impressive thing that happens when you become a priest? Is it celebrating Mass?' Surprisingly he said, 'No. It's hearing confessions, because you share in and act in the person of Christ.' With the Mass and the holy Sacrament we know that the Blessed Josemaria's hands trembled at the thought of picking up the Sacred Host. The idea of touching the Sacred Host made him tremble with awe; this was God he was taking in his hands. It was because of this that we instinctively thought that Don Ricardo would say that the Mass was the most striking experience. But he didn't. He said it was the confessional, and that's my experience too. The habit of saying Mass every day can lead to routine; when you celebrate it you've got to try to remember that Our Lord is there and He's expecting you, His friend, to say something and to welcome Him. He's come down from heaven to earth, and you should say, 'Oh, Jesus, how I love you, I'm glad you've come and I want to take you into my heart, and I'm going to give you to these other people.' Well, that's fine, but in terms of actual happiness and joy, there is more rejoicing in heaven over the one sinner who repents. I reckon that would be the experience of all good priests.

FAITH, HOPE AND CHASTITY

God, somehow or other, gives one a tremendous ability to take confession in one's stride. Some regard it as a traumatic experience. Others come along who are obviously very apprehensive because they think they are unusual. Pride takes many different forms. You get people who are intellectually proud, or people who are proud of their talents as tennis players or singers. But even the humblest person can be proud. A lady in a hospital bed will say to her neighbour, 'You want to see what he took out of me!' – she's even proud of some sort of growth. Now that's extraordinary, the capacity of the human spirit to be proud of some abnormality. It's ridiculous of course, but it's quite often the attitude we have towards our sins. We consider them unusual or unheard of, and yet, as it says in the Old Testament, there is nothing new under the sun.

I wear a cassock pretty well all the time but if people find it odd I tend to pay little attention to their reactions. The Blessed Josemaria arrived in England wearing a clerical suit because at that time priests in this country were not supposed to wear the cassock or soutane. It was actually obligatory in Canon Law but prohibited in English law; this was rescinded a few years ago. But if a police officer had known about this law – which is unlikely – and stopped me in the street and said, 'Hey, you're wearing a cassock,' I would have said, 'Well, I'm guilty, but you'll have to take another 50 million offences into account, because I've been wearing cassocks for the past 35 years, ever since I was first tonsured and ordained in Spain.'

Those priests in the Worker movement in France were very laudable in what they were trying to do, taking off their clerical garb and going into factories to work alongside the men there in the hope of evangelizing them. But it didn't work. They ended up leaving the priesthood, and for every 100 priests only ten or so persevered in their vocation. They were purely seminary-trained and didn't have the worldly experience to resist the temptations. I've worked in a factory as a layman for two years and it's effing and blinding all the time. It's unbelievable what goes on when men are all together, the things they come out with. This shows quite clearly why Catholic lay people who are dedicated to God are the solution to the evangelization of the world. But also, suppose I was a priest dressed as a layman and was working in an office or a factory, and I was young and good-looking and smart, and the young ladies found out that I was a priest. They would be flabbergasted – worse, they'd be horrified. It would be a deception. But dressed as I am, they can see what I am.

We hope to go to more cities in this country. Our Lord said, 'I must go to other towns and villages.' In the early days of Opus Dei, even though the Blessed Josemaria hadn't exhausted the whole of Madrid, he still went to start things up in Valencia, Barcelona, Bilbao, Seville and many other big cities. This is what we ought to do. We ought to make other 'ignition points' as the Father used to say, to give people in other places the chance to encounter Opus Dei. It isn't everybody's cup of tea and there are many other institutions and groups in the Church that are engaged in the re-Christianization of the world. Some of the older ones seem to be fading, but there are lots of new movements springing up, just as in a garden some things decay while others begin to sprout and blossom. Opus Dei does not have a monopoly, but we must reach out to as many people as possible to give them the opportunity to learn about the spirit of the Blessed Josemaria. It may just suit this person or that.

Opus Dei is a tremendous help to living a spiritual life in the middle of the worries of the world because we are continually reminded to keep in God's presence. Our faith depends entirely on God and is characterized by the fact that it is God who comes in search of us, whereas in other religions people grope their way towards God. They're groping, but we already have it. Our Lord is with us; He comes to look for us. Our problem is that we present obstacles to this, we sadden the Holy Spirit, and that's why it's so important to have these devotions, to the Angels for example, for they 'see the face of My Father continually' and so keep us focused with a constant supernatural outlook. We also have the warmth and the comfort that is given by devotion to Our Lady. Sometimes even good Christians complain of being dry or cold in their love of God; this is where Our Lady comes into her own, bringing the warmth of her devotion. You can't beat the Rosary for keeping you on the right track; if you have devotion to Our Lady, you won't lose your way.

Opus Dei is not growing as fast here as in other countries like the Philippines, Mexico or Spain. We've had a bit of stick in this country and there's no doubt it does slow things down. When you get a scurrilous article in a newspaper it upsets parents and brothers and sisters. It's also disturbing to people who might otherwise think that Opus Dei is for them; they have second thoughts when they hear somebody decrying it. That was the Blessed Josemaria's experience at the beginning. He was defamed in his twenties – before he even got going – by his fellow priests who didn't understand what he was doing. He was saying that lay people could also be saints, that they didn't need to be a religious or a priest in order to be a saint, and his fellow priests thought that was heretical. But the Blessed Josemaria's teaching has been vindicated by the Second Vatican Council with its universal call to holiness.

Any sorrows? Well, just as the joy of the priesthood is seeing people responding to the love of God, so the hardest part is the opposite. It's seeing people who have abandoned their vocation and abandoned their calling from God, or others who have come along to spiritual activities, taken an interest in the spiritual life, and then quite clearly gone back to their old ways. On those occasions I feel I have failed, just as Our Lord was saddened when His sayings were too hard and He asked, 'Would you too go away?' Christianity *is* hard – for many it seems impossible; they prefer the easy way, the broad road that leads to perdition. And that's sad.

2. Father Timothy Radcliffe OP

Fr Timothy Radcliffe, Master of the Dominican Order, was born in London in 1945

When I arrived at Santa Sabina, the headquarters of the Dominican Order in Rome, Fr Timothy Radcliffe showed me round the beautiful medieval monastery. Noticing that a door needed to be wedged open but finding nothing readily available with which to do this, Fr Timothy removed his shoe for this purpose and thereby ingeniously solved the problem. Two minutes into our appointment, he was escorting me round the cloisters wearing only one shoe – rather like the children's literary character, Mr Magnolia. It was a spontaneous gesture, at once unsettling and endearing.

After spending a sunny afternoon in Rome with Fr Timothy, Master of some 40,000 Dominicans worldwide, I came away with the word 'great' lodged in my mind. At the risk of sounding obsequious, I believe that Fr Timothy has an intellectual and spiritual grandeur which mark him out as one of the great men of our time. The greatness of Fr Timothy springs precisely from his profound humility – a humility which continually seeks deeper answers and confronts harder questions. His description of loneliness is a case in point. Loneliness, states Fr Timothy, is an element of the human condition which we have to face without fear. 'Don't run away,' he says. 'Don't fill it with alcohol. Don't fill it with food. Don't fill it with power. There is an emptiness and a loneliness which you simply have to live. And if you live it, then it will be filled with God.'

Fr Timothy was once described as an overgrown boy by a world-weary broadsheet journalist. I could not quite banish this

FAITH, HOPE AND CHASTITY

remark, which seemed unfair and yet potentially accurate. It was only afterwards that I realized why. There is something childlike about Fr Timothy – his openness, his intellectual curiosity, his trust. Being childlike, however, is quite different from being childish. The qualities of the child – freshness, receptivity, a willingness to take risks – are gifts which most of us quickly lose. 'And it is to such as these that the Kingdom of Heaven belongs.'

Ultimately we all have to face our sexuality. A clear and explicit recognition of how sexual we are is often avoided when people join religious Orders or seminaries, and yet I don't think we can live in a society where sex is so pervasive without facing sexuality. How do we do this? I think when we look at the role of sexuality in our society, it suffers from a sort of paradox. On the one hand it is the most important thing that there is. On the other hand, it's trivialized. There was an American novelist whose name I forget who said that today, sexuality – sexual intercourse – is the one remaining sacrament of transcendence. It is the one moment when people discover that they really exist and that there is someone else for them. Sexuality for many people has become uniquely important as a moment when they feel valued, when they feel that they have a relationship.

It's very interesting how the English language has changed from 30 years ago, so that to have a relationship with somebody doesn't mean a friendship; it means that you sleep with them. That implies that nothing else really counts. But alongside this enormous value which has been given to sexuality, it has also become trivialized and almost unimportant. I remember reading in a newspaper that Cynthia Payne, the famous madam of South London, said, 'Having sex is no more significant than having a cup of tea.' Now I think this combination makes celibacy particularly difficult because on the one hand it tells you that you have to have sex, but on the other hand it tells you that it's not particularly serious if you do. How do we respond to that? I think we have to say that it's less important than it's said to be, but it's also more important. On the one hand it is indeed a sacrament of transcendence, which is why in fact it's a sacrament of the Church, but it's not the only one; we can encounter both God and love in many other ways. There are all sorts of ways in which we can be people who love, who give ourselves, and who encounter the ultimate mystery of life. So our faith locates sexuality within a much larger perception of our lives. On the other hand, where society trivializes sex, we should grant it importance, and say that it is not just like having a cup of tea, that sexuality touches the most profound parts of our humanity. If you sleep with somebody, then you give yourself to them completely, and that act of self-gift can never be trivialized.

Celibacy is a real loss, one has to face that; it's no good pretending otherwise. But I think it makes sense if you realize that it doesn't mean that you don't love. There are wonderful examples of people like Jordan of Saxony and Blessed Diana. Jordan was the second Master of the Order, Dominic's successor, and he obviously fell deeply in love with a nun called Diana. Their letters to each other overflow with love. It was a love that was not consummated and you could say that maybe that was a real deprivation. But you could also say that it had a depth which some other loves never attain.

I do deeply regret that I don't have any children. I think that as I've grown as a Dominican, and fought the battles of celibacy and chastity with the help of my brothers and friends, I regret not being married more, and I regret not having children more than I would have done 20 years ago. But for me that's *not* a sign that I should have married and not been a Dominican. If anything, it's a sign that religious life has helped me to grow emotionally. It's helped me to mature slowly, in fits and starts and bumps and falls, to a point where now I really understand much more about the beauty of marriage. If I miss it more, it's because religious life has helped me to do that. Paradoxically, as I grow older I miss marriage more but also I am happier as a friar.

Without a doubt I had a happy childhood. I think what was important was that I didn't only have my five siblings and wonderful parents, but also innumerable cousins, so in a way it was a very good introduction to religious life. The house was always filled with people; there were always guests, friends, cousins. I think another thing that was important for me was that I grew up in the countryside. The house was quite isolated and so a lot of my childhood was spent in the woods; a love of nature was a

FAITH, HOPE AND CHASTITY

very important part of my religious formation. The contemplative experience of being in the woods, of learning to listen to the animals and to distinguish between one bird and another was a very important education. You have to learn to listen if you want to be a preacher. In a way it made it odd for me to become a Dominican because Dominicans are people of the city – Dominic immediately sent the friars to the cities. And yet I retain a great love of the country.

People often talk about the Radcliffes as if we were one of the old recusant families, but that is not strictly true. We only came back to the faith a couple of hundred years ago, but then we married into these old Catholic families. I suppose coming from this rescusant background gave me two things that were very positive. One was a strong sense of belonging not just to a family, but to a whole network of cousins, and I think that was quite important. It gave me a large identity; I never felt I belonged only to this little nuclear family, and that helps when you join an Order and find that your brothers and sisters come from more than a hundred countries. A second element is that I appreciate fidelity. It's been enriching to have a sense of a long history which has had hard moments. It's made me see how fidelity to the Church means that sometimes one has to be in conflict with the ordinary opinions of society. I have found myself in conflict with the state as my ancestors had been in conflict with the king. At one stage in my life I was quite involved in the peace movement and we had to look at things like whether or not it was appropriate to break the law. Some people were a bit scandalized that somebody from my background should even contemplate breaking the law, but I think that if you come from a long Catholic tradition, there's nothing particularly scandalous about that. Catholics have had to do that at many stages of their history in this country.

After I left Downside I planned to go to university but I wanted to have a year off to get some experience of the wider world. For the first time I found that I was making friends with people who questioned my faith and who challenged me as to why on earth I accepted these strange things that Catholics believed. It was exciting and it was a breath of fresh air to enter a larger world but the question which arose for me, very powerfully, was 'Is my religion actually true?' It was the first time in my life that I had really had to ask this question of truth and it became very important for me. I began to read a bit of theology, I even began to read the New Testament! It became such a fascinating, passionate question that I began to feel the urge to commit myself to the pursuit and the proclamation of what is true. I remembered there was a religious Order whose motto was 'Truth'. The trouble was I could not remember which Order it was, so I telephoned some Benedictine friends who did some investigation and came back and told me it was the Dominicans. I decided I wanted to be a Dominican before I had ever met a single Dominican in my life. It's just as well they accepted me!

I joined the Order in 1965, a difficult time in the history of religious life. It was the end of the Second Vatican Council and everything was being put in question; it was a time of deep uncertainty, a time when many religious were leaving the religious Orders and diocesan priests were leaving the priesthood. Much of the time in that first year of the novitiate I was not at all sure where it was all going or what it would lead to, but it was fascinating; we had all the excitement and the thrill of the Second Vatican Council, but at the same time a deep lack of clarity as to what religious life might mean. Strangely enough I never doubted that I wanted to carry on. Many of my fellow novices went through agonized discussions about whether they should stay or go, but I always felt that I should be doing the same thing. The issues were so exciting and the friendships I made with the brethren were so strong that I didn't ever really seriously consider leaving.

Orders like the Dominicans or the Franciscans or the Jesuits were always supposed to be in touch with the problems and questions of society and with the evolution of theological and social issues. That increased radically with the Second Vatican Council. Typical of this was something like the Movement of Worker Priests in which the Dominicans were major participants. Priests, particularly in France, Belgium and Holland, left their communities to go and live in the poorest parts of the city, often getting very ordinary jobs like working in car factories in order to try and be in contact with workers and their questions. They wanted

FAITH, HOPE AND CHASTITY

to be closest to those who were most alienated from the Church. Often we left the priories and went to live in the slums.

All that was exciting and it did immense good both for the Church and also for religious life. In the last 10 or 15 years we have been struggling to hang on to that openness, that contact, and yet also to think how we can once again have a clear identity as religious and as friars. How can we retain the creativity – the daring – of those times, while retaining our identity clearly as friars who are heirs to a particular tradition and who have made vows of poverty, chastity and obedience? One of the big debates in religious Orders like ours is between those who believe that to be preachers we must be out there in the street – almost anonymously – sharing people's problems and blending into the world, and those who believe that we must have a clear public identity, perhaps wearing our habits in the street, and living a more traditional religious life. We are still arguing about this and that is good!

I come from a profoundly Benedictine environment which I still love and delight in. Downside is of course a Benedictine school but I also had uncles and great uncles and cousins who were Benedictines at Ampleforth, Fort Augustus and Worth, and I think it is really that love of my Benedictine formation that made me wish to be a religious. It's a love of community life, of liturgy, of silence, and so to become a Dominican was not to reject that Benedictine background; it was my particular way of appropriating something I'd learnt to love. It was primarily a choice of religious life. I don't think that I was particularly attracted to the idea of being a priest. Eventually it became clear that if I made my solemn profession in the Order, the brethren would ask me to be a priest. From the beginning of the Order most Dominican friars have in fact been ordained, but that was not the reason I became a Dominican; ordination was a response to a request of my brethren. This is actually a very old understanding of what it is to be a priest; you are a priest because you are asked to be so by your community. For example, when St Augustine became a Christian, he used to keep away from many of the big cities because he knew that if he turned up, people would grab him and force him to be ordained as their priest. They got him in the end!

Slowly I came not only to accept but to love my priesthood, but that was a slow process. I think it started with having to hear people's confessions because there I discovered the wonder of mercy. It wasn't that I was being wonderful, forgiving them, but that together, in the face of the dramas, the sufferings, the difficulties that people lived, *together* we heard and experienced God's mercy. I think one of the extraordinary things about the sacrament of reconciliation is that you are not there to give mercy so much as to discover Christ's forgiveness with that person. I am with them, as it were, helping them to hear the forgiveness that we both need, and that's wonderful. I was always very moved by an incident in one of G. K. Chesterton's novels in which somebody asks Father Brown, 'How is it that you manage to solve all these murders?' and he says, 'Because I committed them all myself. Until you know that there is no sin that anyone's ever committed that you might not commit yourself, you are still just a Pharisee in your heart.' I think the first powerful experience that I had of being a priest was of hearing the sufferings – the sins – of people, and knowing that I could have done those things too. And sometimes I had. So together we heard the voice of the compassionate Christ and that changed my idea of what a priesthood was. My suspicion – the anti-clericalism that I certainly had in me – was partly a suspicion of people who appeared to put themselves above others. I still find that an understanding of the priesthood which is deeply unattractive to me. In the confessional box I found that that is not how we live the sacrament of reconciliation; it is a sacramental act in which we both participate, mediating the forgiveness of Christ as a fellow sinner, not as somebody superior.

The central vow for Dominicans is the vow of obedience. One has to think very hard about what obedience might mean, particularly in our society which is profoundly individualistic and where the freedom of the individual is of central importance and value. One of the beautiful things about our society is that it has a profound commitment to freedom, so I think the question of what it means to be obedient is unavoidable for religious. Am I giving away a freedom that's properly human? Am I actually betraying something which is central to my human dignity? I have to think about that for myself, and as the Master of the

FAITH, HOPE AND CHASTITY

Order I have to think about it with my brothers. The first thing I would say is that, after all these years in the Order, I have found obedience to be a really wonderful way of freedom. It's not the freedom which says, 'Well, I'll give away control of my actions and let some superior decide.' Rather, it's the freedom to give one's life to the mission of the Order, and that is a eucharistic act. It's the freedom of Christ who gives himself to his disciples. He says, 'This is my body. I give it to you.' So in the first place obedience is a free generosity. Here I am, and I give myself to you – rather like in marriage where people give themselves to each other. I couldn't see obedience primarily in terms of, 'Oh, I'm not allowed to do this any more.' It has to be that radical, unreserved, unconditional self-gift which for me is one way of living the Eucharist.

Secondly, it's very important, certainly in the Dominican vision, that the word 'obedience' comes from the Latin word *obaudire* meaning 'to listen'; the two are deeply linked. Obedience for us is not a mindless submission to a superior. We give ourselves to the mission of the Order and every brother has the dignity and the right to share in determination of what that mission is. Central to our government is the fact that we are highly democratic. We meet in chapters – of the community, of provinces, of the whole Order – so the vow of obedience makes one a brother who shares in responsibility for determining what we will do together. At its base is the requirement to listen to each other and to arrive at what is right by debate, by dialogue, by listening. Now sometimes it may happen in an extreme situation that for example a superior has to say to a brother, 'Well, I know you don't want to go to Korea. However, after much discussion, I'm awfully sorry but that is my decision.' If one's made one's vow of obedience, one accepts that that is an ultimate possibility, but in our tradition that would not be the primary example of obedience, only a possible conclusion. Ordinarily, obedience is exercised in dialogue, in discussion, in listening, and it always has been from the very beginning of the Order.

I think it is urgent that we face the challenge of our vow of poverty. Here in Rome in Santa Sabina, which is an enormous great medieval building perched on the Aventine Hill, I sometimes look out of my window and see people camped on the banks of the River Tiber in cardboard boxes. It makes me feel a hypocrite. *I'm* the one who's made the vow of poverty and here I am living in this vast priory and there they are, exposed to the elements and living only under a bit of cardboard. It would be tempting to spiritualize away poverty and religious Orders often do this. They say, 'Oh well, I may live in this big building but I don't personally own it.' I think that is an evasion. Certainly in the Dominican and Franciscan traditions – the Mendicant Orders – poverty usually does require that you actually lack things, that you don't have everything you might want and that you try to live with very little and in simplicity. I think that this is both difficult and important. In our materialistic society, where there is an unlimited desire to possess things, it is an extremely powerful witness when the brethren and the Sisters do actually embrace a real simplicity of life.

This building is exceptional because it's the headquarters of the Dominicans. Obviously thousands of people come to stay here and we have endless conferences and so that's my excuse! But I would say, as I travel around the world visiting the brethren living in some hundred countries, that mostly they do live with simplicity, and that those who live with simplicity and real poverty are always happier. I could almost say that there's a direct correlation between the degree of poverty and the degree of lightheartedness. You can't be lighthearted if you're weighed down with stuff.

As Dominicans we choose our poverty because it's in the service of the primary aim of the Order, which is to be a preacher. A value has not been put on poverty as an end in itself; we are poor because if you want to be a preacher you have to be poor, you have to be free to leave at short notice, you have to be free to go where you're sent. You can't stagger round with endless suitcases of possessions; you can't have carpets and pictures. The preacher who's at the disposition of the preaching of the Gospel must not have too much. I think also our poverty is important if we are to be in contact with the suffering of the world. If we're to preach the good news of redemption, the good news of the kingdom, then we have to be somehow naked and vulnerable to the sufferings of others. I think to be poor and to live simply is to take away what protects you – the walls that insulate you from the invisible poor who are shut out. We often do not live with that vulnerability.

You can see this dramatically in some of the brethren. For example, there is a brother called Pedro who lives in Paris literally on the streets. He comes back to the priory once a week for a wash and to keep in contact with the brethren but he lives on the streets; he lives like a tramp. He can only speak a word of good news to them if he actually shares their life. There are lots of other brothers who have something of that immediacy of contact, particularly in Latin America and parts of Africa. There's another brother who is a chaplain to the gypsies. He has a small caravan and for nine months of the year he's in his little caravan, travelling with the gypsies in France, sharing their life. When they're arrested, he's arrested, when they're put in prison, he's put in prison. Poverty is about shared vulnerability.

The vow of celibacy is a terribly important thing for us to think about today. Where can I begin? I don't think I can preach about the love of God unless I know myself to be capable of loving and of actually having some experience of love. I think that if you want the challenge of chastity, the first thing to ask is, 'How, as a Dominican, as a priest, am I going to love?' I really would underline that very strongly. St Augustine, who often rather unjustly gets a bad press, said: 'Show me a lover and he will know what I'm talking about. People say, "How can I love God?" Love, and *love* that love, for that love is God.' So it seems to me that whatever chastity is, it cannot in the first place be a repression of a human capacity to love. It would be nonsense for us to be a Church which talked about the God who is love if priests and preachers denied and killed that ability in their lives. I love a remark of Meister Eckhart, the fourteenth-century German Dominican mystic, who said, 'Love is the hook with which the fish is caught, and how wonderful it is to be caught by that hook.'

I think we have to learn how to be people who love honestly. How is this to happen? The first thing is that it must take time. In the formation of young Dominicans – Brothers and Sisters who enter the Order – you have to dare to talk about all the issues, and give each other time to grow in a real purity of heart. If somebody joins the Order and they are, say, bad-tempered, you don't expect them to cure that in ten minutes. Facing that anger will take time. Likewise, becoming chaste takes time, whether for religious, or for married people, or for anybody, since chastity isn't just for religious, it's for all Christians. It also takes a lot of honesty and people will have to face the possibilities of failure. Men and women, religious and married people who are growing into chastity may find that there are moments of failure. At those moments it is vital that you believe in forgiveness, that you believe you can grow, and that you are prepared to talk about it, openly, freely and unembarrassedly with other people and in the first place with your brethren. The great temptation is to fall into a double life and then you have a divided heart. If anybody gets trapped in that, they lose the freedom, the spontaneity, the truthfulness which we're called to, and you can end up by hurting other people very badly.

Facing chastity is inseparable from all sorts of other elements of life. Chastity isn't just a part of your life, a part of your heart; it touches fundamental issues about how you relate to other human beings. In the first place it's an invitation to be unpossessive and not to lay hold of other people, not to have power over them. St Thomas Aquinas says that lust is like the lion who sees the stag only as his meal and I think that's very profound, because it is very easy to look at other people only in order to possess them, to own them, to control them. Sexual possession is only part of a much more profound question about how you can take over other people. It's a particular temptation for priests because priests often give up much – sex, material wealth and so on – but compensate by exercising power over others.

If you want to be chaste – married or religious – there has to be a deep letting-go of the desire to own another, in order to give them the space to be themselves. If you're a religious or a priest, another element which is particularly difficult but also a wonderful liberty, is that you renounce being the uniquely important person for someone else; you renounce institutionalizing a unique relationship with one other person in which you can say, 'She for me is the most important person in the world as I am for her.' To give that up is one of the most difficult things – much more so than sex. You're invited to accept not being the centre of another person's life. You're invited to be peripheral, to be part of the supporting cast. You may love many people and you may be loved by many people and I give thanks to God that there are many people whom I love and who love me. In that sense I have an incredibly rich life, and I hope that every religious and priest has people to whom they are deeply attached. But you cannot claim it as your right. Your relationship always has to be one where you give the freedom to the other person to go away, to forget you if necessary; you don't claim them as your own. Now learning that is hard. It's been hard for me. I know when I look back over my life as a religious it's been one of the toughest things that I've ever had to learn. But you make a little bit of progress and what you discover is the pleasure and the freedom of an unpossessive love of other people.

One cannot cope with celibacy unless one confronts loneliness. I think that members of religious orders are very often inclined to think that if they were married they would never feel lonely. But one of the things that my married friends have taught me is that this is not true, that loneliness is an element of the human condition that everyone has to face. Sometimes you can feel most lonely precisely *with* another person, struggling to find a word that can reach across the barriers, and feeling helpless. This can happen even with someone whom one loves. One has to face being alone without fear and let it hollow out a space inside you. You've got to let that hole be. Eckhart says a wonderful thing: 'Stand firm and do not waver in the face of your emptiness.' That's wonderful. Don't run away. Don't fill it with alcohol. Don't fill it with food. Don't fill it with power. There's an emptiness and a loneliness there which you simply have to live. And if you live it, then it will be filled with God. But you can't fill it yourself and you cannot demand of God that God comes and fills it. God comes as and when He wills to come. When I've felt moments of loneliness, the text that has always meant so much to me has been Hosea 2:16 when God says to Israel, 'I will lure you into the wilderness and there I will speak tenderly to you.' It seems to me you will never hear those words of love, the void will never be filled, unless you stand firm and do not waver in the face of that emptiness.

The greatest joy for me has been my friendships. They've been of immense importance, not just because I enjoy them, but because they're one of the ways in which I meet God. Aquinas said that the love we have for God, the love that He has for us, is friendship. I think that so often people see religion as grim, as moralistic, as hard, as about telling people what they ought to do, or usually what they ought not to do. Sometimes we don't see that at the centre of the Gospel is God's utter pleasure in us. Do you meet that and do you know it when you laugh with your friends? I think that the mystery of the living God is present in the friendships we have. It's there that we meet, if you want, the laughter of God and the friendship of God; it's there that we meet God's pleasure in us.

3. Father Shay Cullen SSC

Fr Shay Cullen was born at Glasthule, Co. Dublin, Ireland in 1943

Fr Shay Cullen, an Irish Columban missionary, has been crusading against the sex industry in the Philippines since 1969. This personal mission has borne fruit in the shape of countless convictions including that of Michael Clarke, the British sex tourism organizer. Fr Shay recognizes that child abuse within the Church is also a problem where the wrongdoing is even greater, he says, due to a priest's position of trust and accessibility within the community. The Church, he says, should be pioneering in the fight against child abuse; instead, he goes on, it cringes in fear from the media and shies away from the problem.

This chapter by Fr Shay Cullen is one of only two in the book which have been written in advance as opposed to spoken out loud in the form of an interview – the other being that of 'Fr John', the gay priest who wishes to remain anonymous. Having never met Fr Shay, I, like his readers, am left to make up my own mind. I need little convincing, however, that Fr Shay is an utterly transparent priest, dedicated to the people he serves and relentless in his pursuit of those who exploit them. To borrow a title from Dietrich Bonhoeffer, the extraordinary German theologian who lost his life in defiance of Hitler, Fr Shay is ultimately 'a man for others'.

One night in the Philippines I left off the white cassock that we wore in the church and went out on the streets. It was a wild scene with flashing neon lights and brawling, shouting crowds of sailors. They were striding arrogantly along the street – some pulling young women into cheap hotels, others fighting and yet others tumbling out of bars screaming drunk, only to be subdued and dragged kicking back to base by the US Navy shore patrol. The shrieking scream of electric guitars pounded out acid rock on to the streets while inside the clubs naked women performed lewd shows. A dozen or so, most of them teenagers, stood on a platform gyrating to the music until a sailor called one of them by number, thereby making her his own for the night. It was like Sodom and Gomorrah.

Once outside again I walked towards the gate of the military base. Shops sold T-shirts printed with obscenities and pornographic pictures; others announced that the only good Vietnam was a 'nuked' Vietnam. One showed a mushroom cloud doing the job on a map of that poor country as the jets sped away into the clouds. 'Nuke them till they glow', the slogan screamed. It was the height of the war; the men were on leave and would soon return to the steaming jungles of certain death in a war for which there was no explanation – none that they understood, anyway. Frightened and angry GIs were letting off their war madness on the weak and defenceless women of Olongapo. Women were murdered, others raped; not one GI has since been brought to trial.

I was offered a child. A shifty-eyed Filipino man sidled up to me, laughing and motioning to his side. 'You want girls Jo, young girls, very young!' I was really shocked. He was holding a small, frail child – no more than 11 years old – by the wrist. He was a pimp offering me a child.

I got back to the peace of the empty Church and sat there for a long while trying to make sense of all this. Our apostolate was purely sacramental. For us priests that scene of human degradation did not exist. Nothing was ever said about it, it was never discussed – but I knew I had to try and do something.

My school days had never been very happy. I remember them as being filled with fear and the dread of punishment, and with snide and sarcastic remarks from the teachers and Brothers. The majority were decent enough and some were actually kind and understanding, but the fact that I was always afraid of one or two of the Brothers made life a misery. I don't know how I continued through school. I developed a rebellious attitude at an early age and resisted in every way I could, but this frequently brought more punishment upon me; the cane was wielded with relish. I felt as though there was no escape, no way out. There was also the leather strap – a thick, heavy weapon of torture which made my hands and legs sting for hours. Most of the punishments were for minor offences like not understanding the lessons or not having the right answers. How could one even think when such punishments awaited an innocent mistake? It was a cruel regime in those days. I had low marks and barely passed my exams.

I don't know if I had a vocation as such, that depends on what a 'vocation' is – a calling, a preference? – everybody's understanding is different. For me a missionary life was an interesting opportunity. The visits of the missionaries were a relief from both the regime of school lessons and the feelings of inadequacy that the school system seemed bent on inculcating. The visitors were different, kinder and more understanding. The life they described in the tropics in far away lands was appealing and sounded like a great adventure for me, away from the scenes in school of humiliation, sarcasm and punishment. If it weren't for my loving parents, I would not have stayed in school. My two elder brothers dropped out and went to England to find their future there.

I wanted to be accepted as a missionary – if only I could qualify. With my rock bottom marks there wasn't much alternative. Only the minimum was required – I just had to pass the leaving certificate examinations. 'Great!' I thought. 'That's all I have to achieve and they might be interested.' So I wrote on the slips of paper that were handed round the class, 'Yes, I am interested.'

I remember one day a Columban Father came to the school – Father Balfe, who was kind, affable and easygoing. My friend Pat McDevitt had an uncle who was a Columban missionary, so he had a special interest in accepting Fr Balfe's invitation to visit the seminary for a weekend and meet the students there. I was in the sixth year and leaving soon so I gladly accepted Pat's suggestion that I go too. We travelled in a crowded bus to Dalgan Park on the outskirts of Navan, Co. Meath, which is about 22 miles north of Dublin.

It was a huge building, like a great monastery. It had a stone frontage topped with a Celtic cross and was surrounded by fields spreading out on all sides. In the far distance the historic hill of Tara was pointed out to me. It was a pleasant weekend. We played card games with the students, went for exploratory romps through the Asia rooms and poked around in huge, carved chests filled with Chinese robes and all sorts of strange and exotic-smelling stuff that had been brought back by the missionaries. Then there was the interview. I wasn't expecting that at all, but a Father Keilt invited us to fill out a form with all sorts of details on it about our family and interests. I wasn't thinking seriously about making any kind of promise at that stage, but it seemed expected of us so I went along and filled out the form while sitting at a long table in a musty-smelling room packed with all these ivory carvings and statues and wall-hangings of Chinese characters.

From an early age I had been an altar boy. It became a place where I felt I belonged; we were respected and encouraged and praised when we did well. It was an influence outside my home that made a positive impression on me, especially considering how negative school had been. School had simply given me the impression that the adult world was one of aloofness, cruelty and oppression. As an altar boy, the church services gave us responsibility, status and something special to do as young kids. Having said that, it didn't make me any less mischievous as a boy. There was nothing very pious about it – I was just as wild as everyone else.

I joined the Legion of Mary when I was about 15. We had simple assignments and good deeds to perform; supervising the newspaper and magazine stand was one of them. Many a frosty morning was spent with freezing toes and fingers outside the church trying to sell newspapers and magazines. We did poorly in comparison with the thriving commercial newspaper seller at the church gate. When he asked us what we were doing we joked that while the news boys were selling the news of *this* world we were selling the news of the *next*. But it did create a challenge, voluntarily to get up early on a frosty Sunday morning and serve the early Mass and then stand hungry and cold on the pavement selling religious magazines and papers. Not many young people do *that* any more.

The example of my parents was not to be overlooked in all this. My mother's voice calling up the stairs for me to get up and not miss the seven o'clock Mass was a constant reminder of duty. I learned that I must do what I had promised to do. The solid and unquestioned faith of my parents had its positive effect in keeping me faithful to that duty. That is the way religious practice was in those days. We learned everything by rote and religious practice was planned, organized and to be followed.

All of that gave me an interest in the missionaries. I had done so badly in school that I had to repeat one year – a final humiliation which almost made me drop out. The class which I joined was very different to the one with which I had previously travelled to the dead-end of failing grades. They were far more studious, intelligent and courteous. I felt more respected and was able to settle down. I stopped copying other students' work and started to do my own instead. I did better in the exams and eventually passed the leaving certificate by a hair's breadth.

I had little idea of what I would do in the future. Getting away to England to work in the pea factories of Grimsby filled my mind with thoughts of earning real money, so with a group of classmates I worked in the factories and took a part-time job in a hotel and bar. The months passed and we heard that the results of the leaving certificate exams were out. There were no graduation ceremonies or anything like that. We all stood round a red telephone box in Grimsby and called Ireland to learn the results. I don't know who I heard it from but I could hardly believe that I had passed. Up to that time I still felt like a failure who would have to repeat the exam so as to get any kind of job at all. The result made other alternatives possible.

Pat received a telegram one day from his sister. It said that a letter from the seminary was on its way informing him that if he was coming he had to be there by 22 September. That form we filled in had apparently made us eligible to join the seminary. We talked into the night and in the end decided to go. There was no deep soul-searching about it since neither of us really knew what it entailed. That week we collected our wages and set off for Ireland and Dalgan Park.

Seven years in the seminary at Dalgan brought about serious changes in my life. My faith became personal; it gave me a direction, a purpose and a commitment, so that over those seven years I found self-understanding and confidence. This is not to say there were no difficulties – there were many. I developed a sense of independence and was seen as something of a loner. I developed my own opinions and expectations which brought me grief and misunderstanding on a number of occasions – to the point where I was considered 'unsuitable' for the priesthood.

I remember one occasion when letters were opened and used as evidence against a friend of mine and it led to his being denied ordination. The trust and friendship between students and staff that was traditionally a hallmark of Dalgan was under threat and I felt the whole thing was downright dishonourable. Something important to us was being lost. With the changes of the Second Vatican Council sweeping over us, such totalitarian practices seemed so contradictory. I made some strong remarks about this, which were interpreted not as an appeal for fair play and understanding but as a lack of obedience and submissiveness to God's will as expressed in the will of our superiors. I found it difficult to subscribe to that concept since the will of men seemed more obvious in all this than the will of God. Besides, here were intelligent, dedicated young men, ready and willing for a life on the missions, and after five years or so of effort and endurance they were simply being told, 'Sorry, you're out.' There were times when a rector judged it better that I too should consider leaving, but despite it all I stayed on.

The missions assignments after ordination were always pinned to a noticeboard in the college hallway. On the morning they went up, crowds would mill around the board to learn where their missionary life would begin and indeed where they would spend the greater part of their lives. I ran my eye down the typewritten sheet and saw it – the Philippines.

As I stepped off the plane in Manila and walked down the steps in that September of 1969, the tropical sun scorched me from a clear blue sky and hit me again as it bounced back from the glaring concrete tarmac. Heat, glorious heat; after the bitterness of Irish winters and rain-spoiled summers this was wonderful. I had arrived.

Driving down Roxas Boulevard, lined with coconut trees three deep and with a shimmering Manila Bay to the left, I felt I had arrived in a tropical paradise. After a few days at the Columban Fathers' house in Manila I was driven to St Joseph's parish in

FAITH, HOPE AND CHASTITY

Olongapo City for my first assignment. I was immediately harnessed to the hectic parish routine – long hours in the hot, stuffy confessional with the buzz and whizz of motorized tricycles outside and poor people unburdening themselves to me in a language I didn't know.

Olongapo was known then as Sin City. It was a honky-tonk town that had grown up around the gate of the huge US naval base. The commercial sex industry was the only work in town, or for the educated and healthy, a job in the base itself. There were about 25,000 Filipinos and 7,000 Americans running the vast facility, which encompassed the huge bay together with a mountain range covered in rainforest. When the Seventh Fleet aircraft carriers and escorts steamed in from bombing and shelling the Vietnamese people, another 10,000 sex-starved servicemen would descend on the 500 or so clubs, bars, massage parlours and cheap hotels. There were an estimated 16,000 women and children working as prostitutes or 'hostesses', although officially prostitution never existed. I was threatened with deportation several times for allegedly defaming the good name of the city by saying that it did.

I heard of the terrible deaths of young girls from botched abortions, the rampant venereal disease, the drug abuse and the breakdown of so many Filipino base workers' families. After a few weeks the Columban sisters at St Joseph's school, who were doing everything they could to build Christian values in the students and help them through their family problems, asked me to help with the more troubled students. I was happy both for the opportunity and for a change of pace. I met students who were filled with hostility and anger after their fathers abandoned their mothers for a bar girl and who were now looking vainly for some meaning to their lives. There were occasional fights and gangs but the vast majority of students were making it with the help of the religious sisters and teachers.

One day a 15-year-old student, Oliver, was high on drugs and threatened a fellow student with a knife. I was called over. He ordered me to stand clear or I would get it. I was able to persuade him to talk out his problems and let his hostage go. I got the knife away from him and heard another tale of misery – a history of child abuse that had led to him running away and getting into drugs.

The work that I do with my staff here at the Preda Centre involves protecting children who have been abused and bringing legal cases against the abusers. Some of these offenders are relatives; others are the cronies of powerful politicians. They have harassed and threatened us frequently and brought charges to try and silence us and close the centre. Despite the surveillance and the critics looking over our shoulders there have never been any suspicions or allegations concerning our motives. The worst the critics can say is that we do it for the donations. We want to get rich! There have been numerous articles and television documentaries on Preda and many journalists and social researchers have come to stay here to get to know the children. If there were any doubts about this work, they would have surfaced by now. I have no such concerns. My life is transparent for all to see; people can form their own opinions.

At first the centre helped young people with family and drug-related problems. We then launched a public education campaign to raise people's hopes for a better life beyond the sex industry. Later it expanded into national and international campaigns to create a more just and loving society. But we started and still continue with the individuals who are abused and abandoned. The bases finally closed in 1992 but our battle against child prostitution and exploitation still goes on, since the local government has brought in sex tourists from Asia and elsewhere. The threats go on too, together with attempts to have me deported, but all have failed.

The Church authorities have also made serious mistakes in ignoring abuse by priests, adopting a defensive attitude and covering up the plight of their victims. This, I believe, is morally wrong and in some cases criminally so. The Church as an institution should be open, transparent and in the forefront of the fight against the abuse of women and children. Its cringing in fear from the media has only uncovered its inability to face up to the truth and take decisive and unhesitating action on behalf of children, while also taking care that there is justice for the accused. Perhaps those church people who are running from reality should question their own attitudes towards sexuality. What must also be kept in mind is that the clergy are a tiny and insignificant minority in the world – although not always in their own minds. In the world of paedophilia they make up a very small percentage, but their position of trust and their accessibility to children renders them responsible for a greater degree of wrongdoing.

I do not believe that celibacy is necessary to be a better priest. There are many more married people who have given their lives working for the poor and the downtrodden. They have died, sometimes under terrible torture, for the sake of justice and their faith. Who are we to say that our sacrifice is any greater than theirs? It is just not so. Besides, to think that we, as priests, are better than others because we are celibate is silly; it ought to become optional one day. To make ourselves into a priestly caste, apart from others, is divisive and arrogant. I also think that we have to realize that priesthood is not only about rites and rituals. It also celebrates the cause of justice, the dignity of the human person and the victory of right over wrong.

Celibacy has never been a problem for me, rather an advantage. It has been a clear choice which provides a unique opportunity to do this kind of work because families and children are not endangered. I have been humanly attracted to certain people with feelings of affection and love, but I know there is a line which I cannot cross. To do so would be to forfeit all that I and my co-workers have worked for on behalf of the oppressed and the enslaved. To become emotionally or sexually involved would be like unfaithfulness in a marriage and would rightly be seen by many as a betrayal and a duplicity; my credibility and honesty would have to be questioned. To indulge in a secret affair is to compromise faith and belief. It is better to be open and honest about it, and if the situation does arise, to retire to another life, knowing that one has given many good years working unselfishly for the community. To do that is in many cases not selfishness but the right and best thing to do. But for myself, who has not yet retired to another lifestyle, I have to remain faithful to the goal. There is nothing especially virtuous in that. Millions of couples remain faithful all their lives; why should we clergy not do the same?

I have an added incentive. We are working against evil forces – the local sex industry and their political patrons. They are out to bring us down, to weaken our work and prey on our children.

To surrender to loneliness and a yearning for affection and tenderness – no matter how natural those longings and desires may be – would be to give in to those evil forces and to fail my co-workers who have stood by me through all the hardships. Such failure would be to give the enemy the very incident they want to splash across the front pages. I just couldn't bring that shame on those with whom and for whom I work. They have been faithful to the cause. I just have to grin and bear the deprivation, if you can call it that. Working for justice, saving children from their abusers, trying to bring about changes in society and meeting small successes brings with it a great satisfaction and joy – it's a different kind of happiness.

This deprivation does not diminish me as a person who lives a celibate life. In fact it leaves me free to share a spiritual and human love of a different kind with those who hardly know what a kind word is. Besides, the needs of the poor, the abused and the outcast are so great that there is no time in the day or emotional energy left over for a personal involvement. If I want that, then I will be open and frank and retire first from this work and the priesthood and then settle down into another life. But that is not on the cards for me as far as I can see.

Everybody has a vocation in so far as they have something valuable to offer in their own way, according to their own ability. Young women, the middle-aged or old people who are ready to serve all have a vocation and a role in making this world a better place – in bringing about the kingdom. The priesthood of the laity is there, recognized by the Vatican Council but left uncultivated, unused and undeveloped. That's the problem with a priestly caste, there's no room for others. How selfish we have become.

Our work must go on. Many children have been rescued from being sexually exploited and their abusers are either on trial or convicted. The British sex tour organizer Michael Clarke offered children for sex for the price of a hamburger. He described women as being like fillies waiting to be mounted and would lead sex tourists to them in a vehicle named the Virgin Mary. I found him on a beach here in Olongapo and brought him to court. He was convicted and sentenced to 17 years. Then there was Victor Fitzgerald, an Australian paedophile who took little girls on his yacht in Subic Bay and abused them there. We caught him and he got 8 to 17 years. The latest is a Japanese paedophile who tied up little children as young as six. They were videotaped and made to abuse one another. We charged him and he was given 42 years in a Manila jail. Most trials take an average of two years.

We have had many more convictions of paedophiles and criminals. In a two-and-a-half year period alone, 420 cases have been brought to court in Olongapo. The US Navy wants to come back to visit all ports and secure immunity from prosecution, but the battle lines in this fight for women's and children's rights have been drawn and there is no going back. I guess the publicity our campaigns have aroused is causing most anger among the abusers and the sex industry operators, but that must be a good sign, a sign that we are making progress.

It is these small victories that help to keep me going despite the disappointments and the obstacles. The sheer extent of the evil of child sexual abuse is what makes me feel really sad at times. But that's no reason to slow down – all the more reason to work harder.

4. Bishop Crispian Hollis

Bishop Crispian Hollis, Bishop of Portsmouth,
was born in Bristol in 1936

The bishop's tale came as a surprise. Moving and unusual, it centres around a relationship with a woman whom he first encountered as a homeless and distraught teenager at an Oxford secondary school. Also at Oxford, but as a chaplain at the University, Bishop Hollis ended up taking her on, and what started out as a case soon escalated into a friendship – the fulcrum in fact around which the bishop's life and ministry has turned, his priestly vows all the while remaining intact.

Touching and rare, this story illustrates the power of unconsummated love. To anyone who has committed themselves to a life of celibacy and chastity, Bishop Hollis' experience is an example of how platonic love can be navigated with tact and compassion together with trust in the protection of God. Honesty, patience and control have all worked over the years to preserve and deepen an alliance which initially seemed so unpromising.

The bishop's own background is rooted in the literary world of Evelyn Waugh and Hilaire Belloc – upper class, English and converted. Nurtured among intellectual friends and a close-knit family, his story begins in Somerset, the springboard for what many would describe as a challenging but ultimately charmed existence.

I grew up in a village called Mells in Somerset where life very much revolved around Mells Manor, the house which was owned by the Asquith family. Mrs Asquith, as she was then, was the widow of Raymond Asquith who'd been killed in the First World War. Her maiden name was Horner, so the family goes back at least to the Dissolution of the Monasteries. Mells Manor was reputedly one of the spoils of Glastonbury Abbey, which was dissolved by Henry VIII. Legend has it that when 'Little Jack Horner sat in the corner', the plum he pulled out was the title deeds of the Manor.

In a curious way, the Manor House collected various literary and political people in the thirties and forties, but not from the political mainstream, more from the Liberal tradition. Asquith himself, of course, was Prime Minister, and was the grandfather of the family, so it had a Liberal tinge to it. I remember the literary gatherings in particular because my father was a publisher and a writer and so was very much involved in the world of Belloc and Chesterton, Evelyn Waugh and Graham Greene. They were an extraordinary generation of Catholic writers; we've got nothing equivalent to them in today's world.

Evelyn Waugh was a familiar face and he came with a reputation for being frightfully rude. He didn't get away with it in our house because my mother wouldn't let him – she'd just say, 'Oh Evelyn, don't be so stupid.' During the last ten years of his life, he used to come up for a glass of sherry at midday on most Sundays. I also remember John Betjeman coming to stay quite often on his way to Cornwall. He and my father would read poetry together and sit up for most of the night, laughing themselves sick. I very dimly recall Belloc as a great mountain of a man in a black suit coming down the steps into the garden; that's all I can remember about him – this must have been in the early forties. To us, they were just ordinary people; they weren't particularly famous names.

As children the parent we knew best was undoubtedly my mother. My father was away in my early years because of the war, and then after the war he was an MP and so was in London for much of the time. This meant that Mother was the communications centre of the family; letters were written by her and to her. Father wrote to us occasionally – usually a postcard and often about money – but we did not see a great deal of him. As children, I think all of us found him difficult to talk to; we did not know quite what to say to him and, perhaps, he didn't know how to talk to us. We all regretted this enormously after he died because we all said how much we would have loved to have been able to chat to him normally. He was actually very proud of his family and he loved us all; he just couldn't express it.

I felt the first nibbling of a vocation in my early teens. Ronnie Knox was a frequent visitor because he lived in the village and said Mass for us on most Sundays in the village chapel. He never preached to us. He used to say 'I don't like preaching in front of my friends', which was a tragedy really because we would have heard some wonderful little sermons.

For schooling I was sent to Stonyhurst, a Jesuit establishment in the north of England, which was why I nearly joined the Jesuits. What put me off was that if I had joined the Society at that time, I would probably have ended up as a schoolmaster and I didn't want to do that. Even though I was very close to the Jesuits whose effect on me had been enormous over the years, I chose to offer myself to the diocese of Clifton as a candidate for the priesthood. Contrary to many people's experience of boarding school, I loved it at Stonyhurst. There was work to do, obviously, but I found it very congenial. I played a lot of cricket and had lots of friends there; it was lovely. Our parents only visited us once a year at school – quite a contrast to today's practice. They used to come up for a long weekend, always around the feast of Corpus Christi, but other than that we were apart for three months at a time and that was not thought to be odd.

I think the first days at school were hard. I was only nine and was leaving home for the first time. I remember my father coming to see me when he was lecturing at Stonyhurst; he popped down to the prep school and I burst into tears. He tried to comfort me but I don't think he really knew what to say. He tried so hard to show his love and affection by spending time with us, and taking me especially to watch Somerset playing cricket, but he found it so difficult to express these emotions. I think his own childhood in a very clerical environment had a lot to do with this. His father was Bishop of Taunton and I'm proud to wear his episcopal ring today.

My first appointment as a priest in the diocese of Clifton was to a place called Amesbury, which is in the middle of Salisbury Plain. If you've heard of it, I should be quite surprised. That sounds a bit arrogant, but I'd previously been in Rome training for the priesthood throughout the Second Vatican Council, at the heart of everything that was going on in the Church, and now, suddenly, I found myself in the middle of Salisbury Plain, in 200 square miles of parish consisting largely of shooting ranges and tank tracks. I came straight out of Rome to be a pastoral priest in a rural area it was quite a contrast! But I learnt some great and very important lessons which I wouldn't have missed for anything. In the end, it's people that matter; where you are is not important. The glamour and excitement of Rome during the Council was important but there are better things around than that. The other sharp lesson I learnt in Amesbury was that a lot of a priest's work can be connected with fundraising. Every night in the parish I had to check the tills in the bar of the club and then set them up for the next morning. I remember thinking, 'What's this got to do with being a priest?' But then, without those resources we wouldn't have built a new primary school or a new church, both of which were badly needed. It was good to learn that there's a side to church life that isn't all smells and bells.

I served one year in Amesbury, after which I moved to Oxford to be assistant to Fr Michael Hollings in the University Chaplaincy. I wasn't particularly pleased to move at that stage because I was happy in the parish and just beginning to be of some use there. At every stage of my life the next move has always been the one I wouldn't have chosen. I think there's a good lesson there somewhere. It means that you're always being stretched and it means you're not responsible for the choice that's been made. Somebody else has thought that you could do this job, so you get on with it and do your best.

Those three years in Oxford with Michael were crucial for me. He lived a style of priesthood that I'd never come across before and which was utterly different from the conventional. It had its obvious basis in the fact that he ran an open house so that people were in and out all the time. It's not the style of many presbyteries now and it certainly wasn't then. As a priest and as a person, he was totally available to people all the time. There was an interaction between himself, the undergraduates and countless others which was quite remarkable. I suppose it's a bit easier to deal with people in that way in a university setting because people do come and go much more, but it is, nevertheless, hugely demanding. Michael gave me an enduring vision of priesthood as being about relationships and not just about function. Pastoral work is all about relating to people.

But there was one other extraordinary lesson to be learned from living with Michael. You can't really be an effective priest if you don't pray. For three years I lived with this guy who was up at 5.30 every morning to pray for an hour and a half. An example like that has to be catching! He taught me by example to see that prayer and priesthood are inextricably linked – and it's not just about saying your prayers, it's actually about being alone and one-to-one with God. I'd hear Michael getting up early every morning and I knew that he would be in chapel for two hours before Mass started. I also knew that he'd gone to bed after midnight the night before and that his bed was a sofa. At some stage, before I ever got there, he'd given up his room to someone who needed it more and then never got it back again. It wasn't comfortable living with Michael; he could be extremely difficult and awkward at times, but then that's often the way with saints. If I'd stayed in a parish rather than going to the Chaplaincy, my lifestyle would have turned out very differently.

A very important relationship started for me when I was at Oxford. One of the student priests, an Australian and now an Archbishop, had been acting as chaplain to one of the Catholic schools in the city. One day he brought a young girl to the house and said, 'This girl needs looking after. Her parents are dead, she's been fostered, she's at the school and she's on drugs. I don't know how to help her.'

The fact that this priest felt he could bring her to us is indicative of the sort of house Michael Hollings had made of the Chaplaincy. We had the girl in for meals from time to time and did the best we could but we really weren't getting anywhere. In the end, Michael and I sat down and said, 'What are we going to do? We're just mucking around at the moment and not actually being of any help at all.' To cut a long story short, we took her into the Chaplaincy and gave her a home. There were others living in the house so it wasn't as if she was on her own with two priests.

Michael moved on two years later and I succeeded him as Chaplain. That move could have been disastrous for the girl because she had a reverence and an affection for him, but I had also become a very steady factor in her life. In fact, I had become the stable relationship for her and it was becoming increasingly clear to me that if somebody did not love her and continue to engage her trust, she would literally not survive.

I did my best to give her that love and trust. It could have been a disastrous course to take, destructive for my priesthood and, perhaps, her life. Thanks be to God, it worked out all right. I was able to engage her trust, which meant in turn that there was no way I could betray her or run the risk of rejecting her. It was a hard but immensely valuable way of discovering the demands as well as the enormous grace and power which can come from faithful celibacy.

She lived in the house for the best part of eight years. We saw her through A levels and then college. She got a place at Oxford University, trained as a teacher and then got a job in a London school. One day she came to tell me that she was going to join a religious community. I think I said something like, 'You must be crazy. With your history nobody's going to take you seriously.' But I was wrong; she was taken seriously and she's now happily living the life of a contemplative nun and has just completed a doctorate.

The relationship has been enormously important to me and very formative for my life as a priest. It has helped me come to terms with my emotions in a very real way, but also in a way that's entirely healthy and proper. We have a very deep and enduring love and friendship today. In many ways, it's the closest relationship I've ever had or am likely to have. The journey has been complicated – even risky – as it has unfolded, but I've always been very conscious that the hand of God has been there and that we have been guarded and protected. It's made all the difference to my priesthood and my life and if I ever needed convincing of the power and creative holiness of the gift of celibacy, then this experience has given me that conviction. To have saved this person from rejection and, possibly, an early death and to have been used by God so that she could live is one of the most important things that has happened to me. It's made all the difference to what little I have been able to do as a priest and to the sort of person I've been able to become. I am more free, more responsible and even, perhaps, a little holier. I am much more aware of my own emotions and the emotions and needs of others and I like to think that I may have become more human.

Questions about celibacy are all around today and many say that the discipline should be relaxed or changed. From all that I've already said, you'll understand that I am not a campaigner in this question. I really believe in the power for good that comes from a celibate priesthood, but I recognize that there are situations where, if I could ordain a married man, a community would be assured of the celebration of the Eucharist. In our diocese at the moment we've got priests in nearly all our parishes, but when they retire or die I'm not sure what I'm going to do because I haven't got anyone to replace them. This worries and saddens me, particularly when there are probably many married men who would make excellent priests for those parishes.

There's a further problem in all this too. In recent years we've lost three or four senior priests who have left because they wanted to get married. At the same time, we've been ordaining former Anglicans who are married. I've personally no regrets about this and those we've ordained have proved to be wonderful priests, but some people find it all very difficult to understand. They say, 'What's going on? These good priests we love want to marry and they've got to leave the priesthood and yet, at the same time, you're ordaining married men. Why can't our priests be married if they want to?'

These are real questions. I know that there is a very clear distinction between the two situations but it's quite difficult to make it understandable in simple terms. Priests who leave to marry did take on a commitment to celibacy; they made promises about it and those promises are being set aside. They really are in a different situation to those married former Anglicans who are seeking ordination.

There's no such thing as a life without sacrifice – everybody gives up something – and in my experience it's very rare to get back less than you've given. We who are ordained give up the possibility of marriage and all the riches that entails, but the very giving up opens up all sorts of other relationships at different levels which would be very difficult for a married man to have in his life. I can give time and attention to people in ways that would be very difficult for a husband with a family. I can give away my time. I'm free in an unlimited way to give myself to anyone else who's in need. I'm not saying that I always do – sadly not – but I am free to do so.

This is priesthood for me and I love it, and I love the Church, with all her faults, in which I've been called to serve as a priest. I can't think of anything that I would rather have done. Certainly it's been difficult at times – even very difficult – and it's always been challenging, but I know, without a shadow of a doubt, that it's what the Lord wants me to be and I am very happy about that.

Being a priest or a bishop in today's Church means being in a pivotal position. It means being a leader – even when you feel you're not very good at that; but you don't have to lead in everything, you don't have to be a 'Jack of all trades'. You've got to lead through prayer and worship and spirituality because that's how you begin to enable others to recognize and offer their gifts. You've got to be the one who gathers the community together to hear the Word, to celebrate the Sacraments and be Christ to our world. I can't think of anything more fulfilling than that.

5. Father David Cullen WF

Fr David Cullen was born at Croydon in 1932

When I first met Fr David Cullen, I expected him to be some-
what apologetic about his life as a missionary. I also assumed
he would reconstruct the whole concept of mission with ample
references to the work of CAFOD, the main Catholic charity
for overseas aid and development. I was startled and surprised
therefore when he did not. Instead, he spoke passionately about
the joys of introducing the Christian faith to people who would
otherwise be pagan. He felt certain that where Christianity did
not exist, evil stepped in to fill the vacuum.

Brought up by parents who divorced while he was still a child,
Fr David lived above a pub with his mother who was a licensee.
He hated the disturbing presence of the pub and remembers how
as the evening wore on, the smoke would rise up through
the floorboards of his bedroom. Relief was found in the form
of a private boarding school where he would spend happy and
secure holidays with his aunts; this was followed immediately
by seminary. While his interest in the priesthood was strong, he
nevertheless found himself dropping out. It was only in Africa,
as a member of the army, that he realized with a shock of recognition that he wanted to be a missionary. A tender man who
spoke with great dignity of his love for Africa and her people,
Fr David opened my eyes to the conviction with which missionary work still operates throughout the world today.

I once went to a completely pagan village where I felt a strong sense of the presence of evil. I can't describe it but there was something in that village that just left me feeling extremely uncomfortable, almost as if it were still in the grip of the forces of evil. Perhaps it was just the absence of even a single Christian that made the atmosphere there so alien to me. Whatever the reason, I felt very uncomfortable.

Our big enemy in Africa is witchcraft. It's so deep in the people that as long as things go all right they remain very attached to their faith and some of them are very strong Christians – they are often great Bible readers. But when things go wrong, like sickness or death, the people believe somebody must have caused it. They think the sick person has been bewitched or poisoned; they don't believe an illness could have natural causes. So the witchdoctor is visited in order to find out who caused the sickness. They use all kinds of funny tricks; they put up mirrors and you're supposed to see the face of the culprit in the mirror ... I mean, they're clever enough. They find out who's got a grievance against you or who you've got a grievance against, and they say, 'That one. He – or she – caused the death of your child.' So then there is an act of vengeance against the accused family and one of their children is poisoned or whatever. That sort of thing is very common. It's the same in the city except that over there the women drive limousines when they go to see these old witchfinders.

We resist this witchcraft very strongly and try to do something about it. We say to the Christian community, 'This is your responsibility. You must care for these people.' We warn them, 'If you go to the witchdoctor, you'll be out – excommunicated' – we have to be as strict as that. People say, 'We only went for the medicine.' 'Never mind,' we say, 'you went to the witchdoctor. Finished.' Of course, there's also what we call 'reconciliation' although the people call it punishment. We have a week in an outstation for people who have been excommunicated. The catechist gives them instruction and some manual work and then at the end of the week people go to confession and we have a Mass. Oh, they're so full of joy! You see, they can receive communion again. Other people take part in these 'refresher courses' as well: girls who have had a baby out of wedlock, second wives – people who are living in irregular situations.

I once went to a village chief who showed me some of the witchdoctor's tools. There was a plane carved out of wood. The people believed the witchdoctor actually got into that plane and flew around. They believed the witchdoctor, in his own way, could usually fly. I mean, we can never truly understand everything that goes on. We try to enter into the African mentality but it's difficult for us; we're always foreigners there. Even as good missionaries with a good grasp of the language and customs, we're still second-best because we'll always be foreigners. They're orientals, we're occidentals.

They also believe the witchdoctors need human limbs, which is why they sometimes want people killed; there is a terrible fear of these witch-hunters. Their job is to pick out the 'witch' who's caused the sickness or death or whatever it is. Very often it's elderly women who are picked out, sometimes a whole village. The chief – the headman – will call in a witch-hunter and say, 'We've got some witches here in the village because there's been a lot of sickness and death.' Anybody who refuses to go is already suspect. You have to be a very strong Christian not to go and have this trial by ordeal. Many Christians fall that way; sometimes a whole village has to be cut off from the sacraments. It's strange but when elderly women are named, they often say 'Yes, I am a witch' and they're expelled from the village ... ostracized. They have to try and survive somehow on the edge of the village. Perhaps it's a psychological thing – somehow they think, 'Yes, it must be me who's the witch.' I remember one occasion when a leper had been excluded. His name was Joseph and we used to go and visit him outside the village where he'd been made to live. One morning someone went to his little hut and there he was – dead. Somebody had killed him. It always makes me think of the scene in the gospel of St Mark when the leper dared to approach Jesus, even though he was not meant to come anywhere near the community as his fellow Israelites believed he was a sinner receiving his just punishment from God. Likewise Joseph had been forced to leave the village and live on his own, ostracized by the community.

People are torn between the traditional things – the animism that's been going on for thousands of years – and the Christian message which is very demanding. I see some wonderful Christians in Africa who live in what I think are model Christian communities. I also meet wonderful pagans who I can speak with about God and that's marvellous. But, you see, the witchdoctor brings evil because he – or very often she – divides families by causing acts of vengeance. But it's all hocus pocus stuff as far as I'm concerned.

Most of us drive pick-ups in Zambia so that we can perform the duties of bus, ambulance and hearse driver. I had a baby born in my car once but I was told to push off by the women, because men mustn't see these things. I have taken children to hospital and they've just died there. It's one of the hard things ... you're absolutely dead tired and people come knocking in the middle of the night and yours is the only car around. It's very difficult to say no, especially since if I do say no, they end up carrying the sick or putting them in a little rickety cart. I find it very distressing but I just can't say yes to everyone, otherwise I get completely flaked out. One time I did delay a little bit. This woman was sick and her husband said, 'Can you take her to hospital?' 'Well,' I said, 'let's have a look at her.' As far as I could see, she wasn't too bad. I thought it was malaria so I gave him pills and said, 'Let's see how she is in the morning. Come and see me then.' She died that night. It's a dilemma because our policy is very much to have a church that's self-helping, self-supporting and self-propagating. In fact, it works very well to a large extent and I would hate to be called paternalistic – that's a dirty word and if you're too much of a soft touch, you can be accused of that. So I'm torn in half sometimes.

In the rural parish in Zambia where I worked, in the diocese of Chipata, there are nine outstations and in each station there's a trained catechist. He's given a good house and a garden for himself and his family; he's a sort of kingpin in that area. There's a big outstation church which is fed by, say, six or seven small Christian communities. One by one those small communities build their own little churches made of mud and straw and we train leaders to start taking Sunday services. For five Sundays out of six they do their own thing and run their own show. Somebody is selected as an elder, somebody to instruct the children, somebody to keep a special eye on the poor and the sick, and somebody to lead the services.

If I asked African Christians I know, 'Do you regret that we came?' I'm sure they would all say, 'No, thank God you did come. We love being Christians.' They value it. They find that being members of a Christian community is something wonderful; the Bible sells like hot cakes there. They love being members of things like the Legion of Mary and the St Vincent de Paul groups. They love the liturgy and the youth movements and everything – where there's a strong Christian group there's a kind of joyfulness.

African people take on Christian values and can often fail, like the rest of us, but even if they slip up badly, somehow they still want to belong, they still remain committed. That sense of belonging is very strong and that's why it's pretty painful when they are cut off from the sacraments; they really do long to come back.

We have problems with some of the African priests. I haven't actually seen a priest living with a woman but there have been accidents – children have appeared. Nevertheless, there are many others who are exemplary and who struggle very hard. Celibacy is not in any way part of African culture. In traditional African societies there is no such thing as platonic friendship. If a man and a woman are alone, there's only one reason for it. Even for us, if we visit a woman, we have to leave the door open. I think it's difficult for diocesan priests; they don't have the support of a religious community. In the bush, you see, there's nothing to do and an African priest on his own ... well, I think he needs to be an angel. There's no cinema, no TV, nothing and the women are not slow in coming forward. I think that in Africa we would have a much stronger spiritual base if we had a married clergy. Personally I think I couldn't survive if they said, 'Now, you live in the bush and we'll leave you on your own.' 'OK,' I'd say, 'if you give me a dispensation from celibacy.'

Celibacy is a struggle for me but I still believe it is a gift and a grace and the older I get, the more I see the relevance of it. I suppose in our early days it was seen as part of the package, and also as the hardest thing that was asked of us. I've remained innocent, even through the army – God preserve me; I'm sure that was God taking care of me. I do see a great value in what I would call the 'celibate lover' – not too loving but not too celibate. There's no point in being physically celibate but hard and selfish. For me to be a happy celibate, I have to put people first. That's the ongoing challenge.

I wouldn't ever judge African priests because I think they've been yanked into this. We've imposed our model of priesthood and yet almost all the actual missionaries in Africa have belonged to religious Orders or missionary societies and these have provided a great deal more support. I don't think diocesan African priests are given sufficient support. They're very social people and they need company. They do struggle hard with celibacy but I would be lenient with them if they failed.

The Church in Africa is a young Church. The majority of people are young people – they're not cynical. Of course you get lapsed Catholics and problems and infighting, but it's a joyful Church. We have Bible study days when we hire a lorry, stuff about 150 young people in and go off to the Poor Clares or some other religious house which has a large enough area for us. We'll have mornings where we touch on real problems for them and get all kinds of discussions going. We'll then have a very lively Mass followed by games and things in the afternoon. We also have retreats and in this way we gradually build up young Christian communities.

I think the most rewarding thing is when churches in Africa become self-sufficient, and when the people run the parish and it becomes *their* church. We are there giving our service as priests, but it is their church and they take responsibility for it and they, if you like, take care of us as their priests, rather than us being paternalistic and coming in from outside with all our riches. I find it wonderful when it's like that.

We try to work against the witchdoctors because they're evil; they cause fear, anxiety, hatred and everything that's wrong. So for me this idea that we should have left the Africans alone – that they were quite happy before the missionaries came along – is rubbish. People in Zambia are delighted to be Christians and they celebrate Christianity with a real sense of joy.

6. Father Oliver McTernan

Fr Oliver McTernan was born in Leitrim, Ireland, in 1947

Fr Oliver McTernan is my own parish priest and as such I felt slightly apprehensive about interviewing him. I should not have worried, for as soon as we started recording I sensed his professionalism. As a gifted communicator who regularly graces the waves of BBC Radio 4 on 'Thought for the Day', Fr Oliver is also a unique and much loved priest. For myself as a mother of five, his style of worship has been a godsend. Every Mass is packed, but none more so than the family Mass at ten o'clock on Sunday mornings. Children of all ages sit, sprawl and clamber at Fr Oliver's feet while, with one eye on the adults, he leads the children in imaginative and inevitably informed discussions on the readings from Scripture. The children then gather round the altar to say the Lord's Prayer before one of them is chosen to lead the congregation in the Creed. There is a lot of movement in the church and a lot of noise. It's very similar in fact to a mosque or a synagogue, where the communities recognize that children are a vital and, almost by definition, lively part of the service.

Fr Oliver talks with great feeling in this chapter about the parish which he has run for nearly 20 years. He also puts forward a strong case for making celibacy optional and speaks openly about the problems and pain which the rule causes – in his view needlessly. 'I would be a better human being,' he says, 'if I were married and had a family. And if I'm a better human being I'm a better priest.' Perhaps it is just because he is my own parish priest, but such a state of affairs is very hard for me to imagine.

I don't regret not marrying but I miss it. I would be a better human being if I were married and had a family, and if I'm a better human being I'm a better priest. Although I'm more available at the moment, I think the quality of my giving would be richer if ... Maybe it's dreaming, but after years of giving retreats and listening to the journeys that priests make, I think it's a dream that I wouldn't be alone in having.

Celibacy is a canonical requirement. Homosexuality, divorce – all of these things are to do with faith and morals, but a rule like the celibacy rule cannot become an article of faith. It's a valid option for those who want to live the ministry in that way, especially people who live in a religious community, but if celibacy were optional I think the Church would be greatly enriched. We have 100,000 ex-priests at the moment worldwide. How in God's name can we say we're serving the Church when we've got men who are trained, experienced and often still willing to serve the Church, but who are not allowed to because of this human-made law? St Paul himself says, 'My thoughts on this aren't from God, they're my personal beliefs and feelings', so I feel very strongly that the Church must face this option without fear.

There is an aloneness I experience which is different from loneliness. Any priest will find that he longs for space. Your life can be so busy that you truly don't have time for loneliness. But there is an aloneness. I engage with people at various stages of their life. I see the tragedies and the good points and I'm not able to share that at a deep level with someone else; that's a missing dimension in my life. Not being a parent is another missing dimension to my life – a God-given dimension that is under developed – and I have to accept that.

I remember my first confession as a young boy in Ireland. We had to go and practise with the brother who was teaching us and he was a rather sadistic type. I remember that I got something wrong, whereupon he came out from behind the screen and into the confessional and gave me such a whack across the face ... and then just left me. I was too frightened to come out so I stayed in there for what felt like an eternity. Eventually, after being locked in the church, I was found by the cleaning ladies.

After an event like that I could say, 'Well, if this is religion I want nothing to do with it', but thankfully I found that things like that never got in the way of my own faith and I would put that down to my father's example. He had a very strong faith and I sensed that belief in God transcended the Church, so that I could acknowledge the failures of the Church without having a crisis of faith. I could truthfully say that all through my life I've never had a crisis of faith in God. I've had many crises about the Church but that's something different.

The seeds of my vocation began when I first started to go to Mass as a child. My father took me to Mass and it was then very much a thought in my mind that this was something I would like to do. I wouldn't describe my father as a pious man but I think he was a deeply religious person with a strong faith. You have to think your way back into the fifties when the Mass was a big community event. There was a sense of something sacred going on, a sense that this was something unusual. It wasn't part of your day-to-day experience. And all of that was in the context of a life that was lived in faith. I mean, every day the Angelus bell would ring and we'd say the Angelus whether we were in the classroom or the playground, so our whole life in that fifties Irish community was faith-orientated.

At the age of 18 I went to an English-speaking seminary in Lisbon to study for the priesthood. There was a very harsh regime there. We had to wear clerical dress all the time, even in the street, and were never allowed out on our own. We were only able to leave the seminary once a week and then always in twos. I think Bishop Butler described it well. When I came back from Lisbon he said, 'It sounds as if you've had all the disadvantages of monasticism and none of its advantages, namely that you can re-elect your superior.' We weren't allowed home for two years, so even our holiday period was spent with the same people. They also had this ridiculous system of seating us according to seniority, so I sat next to the same people for two years – in lecture rooms, in the chapel and in the refectory. I found the whole seminary experience quite off-putting and in some ways damaging; one had to fight against it to survive. We had no chance of change, we were just caught in a system. I really do see those years as a time of missed opportunity.

I was ordained in 1972 and was first appointed to a parish in Islington in London. This was something very new because it was inner city and I was plunged into all sorts of problems that none of my training had prepared me for. There were a lot of social problems, such as housing and family breakdown. Also we were never trained in the seminary to organize our time or to identify priorities and we weren't really given the spirituality to cope with the unpredictability of parish life. One of the problems for the secular priesthood today is that we don't have a spirituality that sustains us in our parishes. Of course I could carve out time for my own prayer life, but that would mean having to distance myself in many ways from other people. I think the much more challenging question is to find a new kind of spirituality that doesn't depend on a person being selfish or being in complete control of one's own time.

Last Sunday's Gospel is an excellent example of that. Jesus said, 'Let's get away for a time, we need to have rest, we need to have prayer.' They go off and what do they find? They find the crowd. But Jesus didn't say, 'Well now, sorry you lot, this is my time. I need it.' He addressed the needs of the crowd. And I think that's the challenging type of spirituality that secular priests have to incorporate into their daily ministry.

The most Christ-like person I know in terms of ministry is a mother. I was watching her last Sunday at Mass. She came to Mass needing time and space and yet her children were constantly wanting her attention. Through the whole of that time she had two qualities: accessibility and availability to her children. And I think those are the two things that we see most in Christ's life. She had to spend the whole Mass being alert and aware of them, as they climbed over this or fell on that or whatever, and she had to respond. It's that spirit of total self-giving that we have to try and develop in our secular ministry because in the process of giving one is actually enriched. There are things that crop up in parish life which mean that you just cannot say 'Well, I've got to say my prayers so I'll deal with that later', because actually your encounter with Christ and your spiritual growth can be in the middle of that crisis.

I became parish priest of Notting Hill in 1980 so I've been here for almost 20 years now. Any parish community by definition has to be all-embracing. For whatever reason, many people are damaged and we have to be patient and compassionate, and overcome any feelings of embarrassment we might have at being associated with people who are clearly neurotic. But it's also part of the responsibility of a minister to ensure that if someone is damaged they're not spreading that on to others. I have to exercise a certain discretion in how I incorporate people into parish life. At times I have to challenge people; there needs to be a direct confrontation but done in a compassionate way. That is probably one of the hardest roles of being a parish priest. By nature I would like to run away from any kind of confrontation and yet I see that if a community is to develop and grow there is no way I can avoid it.

On a personal level I also make it very clear to people that I'm not a substitute psychiatrist. My role is purely to help them spiritually, in terms of the expectations of the Gospel. If people try to use me as a substitute for their psychoanalyst, I usually draw the line very quickly and say, 'Look, that is something I cannot address. It would be irresponsible.' What I can do is help people understand that their problem doesn't isolate them from the love of God, and doesn't prevent them from having a meaningful and mature spiritual life. That for me is the role of the priest. If you ever take a group of pilgrims away, you soon realize that not everyone walks at the same pace, not everyone sees the same things. Some people need much more attention and caring, others are more independent-minded; they go off and explore and come back and enrich the groups. Others need you to hold their hand the whole way. That's a powerful image of what our parish community should be like.

The test of our Christian faith is whether it bears fruit in our ordinary day-to-day lives. You can have people who only go to Mass on Sundays but still get enough spiritual sustenance to go out and give first-class witness to Gospel values. They could be living a truly sacramental marriage for example; their day-to-day encounters are enriching and they're doing the corporal works of mercy. The problem is, there's always a tendency to form a 'holy huddle'. It's an unresolved tension in the life of the Church between faith isolating us from ordinary day-to-day life and faith actually inspiring us to fully engage in ordinary life in a way that can make a profound difference to the world. My vision of faith is very much the second one. We should be enabling people to work within their sphere of influence and to change that. That means that at parish level we've got to have a broad-based community. If a person can only spare an hour a week, or a month, they can come and use that hour profitably either in Mass or by doing something in addition for the parish. They shouldn't feel guilty about only giving an hour. They still belong to the parish as much as the person who can give several hours a day.

In this parish we have not suffered a decline in Mass attendance over the years – in fact it's increased. Having said that, there are Masses I've gone to when I've been on holiday which, were I subjected to them on a regular basis, would have made me give up. I've been to Masses where there was no attempt whatsoever to engage the community and people were obviously just going out of obligation, and not out of a desire to pray. Moreover I fear there's been no attempt to analyse what's been happening; we've been looking at this trend nationally for a long time but we haven't addressed it. We haven't once said, 'Why is this happening? What are we not communicating? Are our Masses really a celebration of God's word and the Eucharist?' The bishops just haven't thought about it because we've had waves of immigrants from Catholic countries who have filled up the pews and staved off the problem; we haven't seen the crisis that is now looming.

One of the biggest problems here in Britain is that we've had no pastoral planning. We have never sat down together, priests and laity, with our bishops, and worked out the most effective way of communicating the Gospel and sustaining our own life in the faith. We had the Liverpool National Congress in 1980 but no follow-up. That Congress gave a wonderful vision of how the Church in Britain needed to develop its own spirituality in order to enable people to witness to the Gospel, and yet it became a closed book. If any parish is to grow and develop it needs to have some sort of pastoral plan: Where are we now, where are we trying to go and how are we going to get there?

Celibacy is a sacrifice, but it can also make one extremely selfish and that is often not recognized. We don't have the day-to-day challenge which an intimate relationship calls for, especially a marriage and parenthood. I truthfully think that if I were married I would be a better priest. Some very good Orthodox priests have lived their ministry in extremely difficult circumstances –

I'm thinking particularly of the Communist days – but have been enabled by their commitment to their family to be good priests and give good witness. It's not so much the quantity of service one gives as the quality of service. I'm not saying that celibacy is something that in itself should be ruled out. Far from it – I think it's a valuable option. But to close down the priesthood to the vast majority of Catholics simply because we're not prepared to look at the celibacy issue is very shortsighted. It shows a lack of openness to the changing needs of the Church and the promptings of the Spirit. I'm not saying we should encourage priests to run out and get married – we'd probably be very bad husbands because of the way we've lived our lives without that personal, intimate challenge of a relationship. But why not open up the priesthood to people who are married and who are capable of doing both jobs?

I think the priesthood has to reflect the whole of life and so there must be a place for gay priests as well, provided they live with integrity and within the acceptable norms of the Church. The Anglican Church is much more honest and open about this than us. We might also say they're more naïve but at least they put things on the agenda and discuss them; we don't deal with things in the same open way. Paedophilia, for example, was a major problem in the Catholic Church for a long time but was never dealt with openly. The media forced the issue out into the open and the scandals forced the bishops to act; there wasn't an internal concern of the Church for the wellbeing of our communities.

Christian ideals are not necessarily the same as ways of living. The ideals are love, integrity, honesty and living the corporate works of mercy, in other words letting the fruits of the Holy Spirit be incorporated into one's life. For 300 years or more of the Church's early existence celibacy was a personal option; it was never seen as a condition for ministry. History seems to indicate that the Church was more concerned with property, Church order, obedience and mobility. For all these reasons celibacy became compulsory in the Western Church. We cannot then conclude that it's the ideal. Likewise, the experience of the Orthodox tradition, where celibacy is restricted to bishops, means that the Vatican Council could never say that celibacy was an integral part of Catholic priesthood.

The hardest thing for me is the constant demands on my time. I'm by nature a very private person so I find it difficult constantly having to be with people. That's the hardest dimension of parish life. But it's more enriching than difficult: living in London and encountering all sorts of people and problems is personally very enriching. I feel I have a very privileged position in people's lives and journeys.

Having spent my whole ministry in two parishes, I firmly believe in parish life. I think it would be a mistake to dismiss it; it's a very good way of living our Christian faith. But the limits of parish life have to be recognized. People's prime purpose in life is in the big wide world and the parish exists to help people live a more Christian life, whatever their condition or job. It's easy to have a circus with lots of activities but that doesn't necessarily mean you are making much impact on changing the world. The most important focus in a parish is the school. We need to give children a solid education and an experience where they find themselves valued and respected, and so have a real sense of God. Then when they move on they've got something that should enable them to cope and grow, wherever they are.

I truly believe that the essence of priesthood is to be of service. It's not about status. I'm wiser now in so far as I recognize that not everything I would like to see happen in the parish is possible, simply because we don't always have the time and resources to implement all our plans. I see my main task now as trying to be a positive influence in a few people's lives. If I can share a bit of a person's journey, give them a sense of where they are going, where God is calling us, then they can go off and hopefully the contribution I've made will bear fruit in their own lives. That's how I would see my ministry now. It's very limited. One casts the net wide but can only touch a few people in a meaningful way. But sometimes the odd word, the odd half an hour, can actually have a major influence in a person's life – more so than if you spend your time caught up in administrating a centre or running this or doing that. Now, if someone wants something, I will always give priority to the individual encounter.

7. Father 'John'

*Fr 'John', a gay priest who feels that he must remain
anonymous, was born in Bolton-le-Sands, Lancaster in 1946*

*I found Fr 'John', who wishes to remain anonymous, a tortured
soul – hauntingly so. A gay priest, now in his fifties, Fr John is
clearly a good-looking man, but is also gaunt and craggy-faced.
His relief when I asked him whether he would like to smoke during the interview was palpable, although the interview itself was
something of a disaster. My machine recorded only part of our
conversation, which meant that Fr John had to write up the
missing section in his own time.*

*The result of our meeting is an account of his own sexual and
spiritual development which is both raw and disturbingly honest.
Moreover, his condemnation of the Church's teaching on sex is as
fierce as his pride at being gay. Both are fuelled by anger and a
determination to celebrate his own homosexuality. Even more
disquieting is the fact that Fr John is now a priest and as such
physically embodies the contradictions between what the Church
teaches and what he – at least in the past – has practised. Only at
the very end of the chapter does he try to square his homosexuality with his Catholic Christian belief – a wretched task that will
convince only some of the people some of the time.*

'Why can't my mother and father just be nice to each other, and
say sorry, and forgive each other?' This was a question which
puzzled me as a tiny child. Probably as a result of my insecure
childhood, I grew up with an intense moral sense. I also had a
deep compassion for the underdog – any underdog. I vividly

remember becoming aware of the horror of Auschwitz when I was about eight, and finding such a level of cruelty unbearable. I realized, even at that age, that in a universe which is mindless, suffering and brutality would not have any final significance. I had a need to believe in a caring God long before I had had much experience of religious belief or practice. It is a conviction which remains in my heart to this day.

My parents were poor; my father was a draughtsman and my mother didn't work after marriage. We lived in a dilapidated and untidy pre-war semi where my parents were actively unhappy. There were many rows and fights and, when I was six, one separation when my father left home for several months. My mother used me as a 'father-confessor' from the earliest times I can remember – that is, she poured out her troubled heart to me concerning the awfulness of her life and the failure of her hopes. My father was usually out of the house, building boats at the bottom of the garden and keeping out of harm's way. My childhood, therefore, was quite unhappy and very unsafe. Nonetheless, each of my parents loved me and I knew this. The neurotic mix of self-confidence and insecurity, assertiveness and timidity, pride and shame, self-love and self-hate which I carry to this day doubtless comes from the complexity of my emotional life as a small child.

My parents were conventional Anglicans of their time. They rarely went to church (my father never) yet they approved of the Church of England and, at some level, had no quarrel with the basic tenets of Protestant orthodoxy. Like most people of the day they thought that Catholicism was rather 'funny' or weird although my mother, rather inconsistently, combined this conventional attitude with an approval of the fact that intellectuals such as G. K. Chesterton, Evelyn Waugh and Muriel Spark had all become Catholics.

I started to go to church because I had a good voice. At the age of nine I was simply told by my Church of England primary school to join the church choir; I have never stopped worshipping since. But I gained more than a mere taste for worship by my membership of the village church choir. I learned how to read music and sing in parts, and my lifelong love of classical music started there with deservedly forgotten nineteenth-century Anglican anthems and short organ pieces performed at Christmas.

I acquired a knowledge and a love of the Prayer Book and the Authorized Version of the Bible, and a lifelong love of good English which is at least partly grounded in that experience.

Above all, I loved the 8 a.m. Communion service which I began to attend after I had been confirmed. I liked the fact that there was no music and no sermon – no entertainment or instruction to justify the activity. It implied to me that God was a reality and that worship of Him was a valid activity. I have never stilled that feeling of wonder. Through the influence of a friend whose father was a high church vicar, I started shedding folk-Protestant prejudices and acquiring a taste for the Catholic way of looking at things. Of High Church ritual I knew little; I never attended a High Church Anglican service until I went to university.

Throughout the time that I was singing in the choir and attending Holy Communion, I was becoming aware that I was homosexual. Gradually, from about the age of six until puberty, I discovered the facts, more or less, about sex, and I also learned something about queers, pansies, jessies, nancy-boys and the loathing and contempt which one ought to feel for them. With mounting anxiety I hoped that I would grow out of my own homosexuality, but as it dawned on me that I probably wouldn't, the one moral concern, even obsession, of my teenage years was how to control or, preferably, extinguish my sexual drive and break the sinful habit of masturbation.

I was, superficially, a successful teenager, with good friends, including girlfriends, and a lively social life with people of my own choosing. And yet I carried the knowledge of my homosexuality as a terrible burden. It was hard, almost impossible, to acquire any reliable information. There were no role models, nor was there any dissemination of ideas sympathetic to homosexuality. Everything conspired to assure me that life was not worth living if you were queer. I was deeply miserable and increasingly without hope as my 'passing phase' failed to pass. Apart from one quick fumble with a man when I was 19, I had no sexual encounters. I abandoned the possibility, let alone the right, to sexual pleasure for myself, and hoped merely to be able to 'go through the motions' well enough with a woman to be able to marry and have children. It infuriates me to think how ignorant youngsters were allowed to be in my day – and possibly still are – about the important aspects of sex. I even split off the emotion of falling in love from sexual desire. I fell in love with girls and fantasized about kissing and caressing them, marrying and having children. Yet anything explicitly sexual, anything genital, was solely concentrated on men – mainly youths of my own age at school or television stars. For men, however, I was unable to feel tenderness. Chatting up, kissing, 'going out' with men seemed repulsive and unnatural; it took me a while, years later, to un-learn that.

I left home to go to university. There I encountered Anglo-Catholicism for the first time and I fled from it. Ignorant as I was about the world, I nonetheless intuitively picked up the connection, which still exists, between High Church ritualism and homosexuality. The thing I most dreaded was that anyone should suspect that I was homosexual. To be associated with Anglo-Catholicism was, I feared, as unwise as wearing a badge proclaiming my sexual orientation to the world.

Exposure of my sexual nature was the most terrifying thing I could imagine and so Anglo-Catholicism was far too dangerous for me to be associated with. Yet I still had strong needs for a Catholic form of religious expression. Several aspects of Catholicism worked subtly together to make it a necessity for me. Its liturgy was a controlled context in which it was safe to feel emotion because it was a well defined, time-limited, other-worldly context. It could move me to tears. In other contexts I rarely cried. 'If you start to cry, what reason is there ever to stop?' was the question which came to me from my underlying depression. Confession offered release – at a price – from constant guilt, and even, so it claimed, a means of building up the soul to resist temptation. This, combined with other rules, requirements and devotional aids, induced me to believe that Catholicism, and only Catholicism, could control my strongly insistent sexual impulses. Finally, it provided me with a seemingly coherent system with which to condemn homosexuality as immoral. I had to do that, for to act upon my sexual promptings would risk my sexuality being uncovered, and that, I believed, would lead to social death. Remember, people were still put in prison at that time, even for private and consenting homosexual acts. Nonetheless, I wasn't a fool. I could see that sex between men didn't actually cause harm to anyone, and yet, if I allowed myself to entertain that line of thought, I knew I would weaken the barriers I had erected to prevent myself from falling into temptation. Catholic moral theology – of a sort which I now despise – at least partly convinced me that homosexuality was morally wrong. It thus deterred me from looking for sex – sex which I both longed for and dreaded.

In the early 1960s Catholic churches were still full and were attended by all types of people. Many practising Catholics were working class; men, young people and families were all to be found in plenty at any Catholic Mass. The one place in England where, as a closet gay, you could safely be a practising Christian was in the Roman Catholic Church. So in my first term at university I approached the Catholic chaplain. I thought, and still think, that if you are a Western European who is convinced by the truth of Christianity, the Catholic Church is your natural home. Also, I have never, in all my time as a Catholic, thought about returning to the Church of England. Nowadays I find it less necessary to convince myself that I believe out of pure and disinterested intellectual conviction. We deceive ourselves if we deny the cultural and psychological elements which lead us to hold the convictions we do – convictions, usually, that we also find congenial.

The Catholic chaplain at the university I attended instructed me over a whole year. We became very close and I respected him enormously. I still do. Yet all the things in the Catholic Church that I most needed at that time – its dogmatic clarity, arcane liturgy, effective discipline and subculture-creating rules such as Friday abstinence from meat – were precisely the things about the Church that he found most irksome. By the time I became a Catholic, I had learnt to distrust all the things about the Church that, psychologically, I most needed. I have never since been able to espouse the whole conservative package or hanker after the more ugly or absurd aspects of the Tridentine Church as it still was then – just – when I became a member of it. For example, I have never thought it justifiable that Mass should be celebrated in a language that no one speaks and I have never given internal assent to the more outrageous prohibitions of the Church in the area of sexual morality.

More important than the chaplain's gift to me of a critical, Vatican II understanding of the Catholic faith were his words to me at my first confession. I now have a great distrust and distaste for the beans-spilling, show-trial aspect of confession as it was then, and according to Canon Law still should be. I was utterly terrified of making my first confession because of one ten-minute session of mutual masturbation which I had taken part in over a year before – the only sexual act with anyone else which I had performed to that point – and which, of course, to avoid a sacrilegious confession, I had to mention. I had never revealed my homosexuality to another soul and nor did I wish to do so. Nevertheless, with shame and trepidation, I spoke of it. The chaplain said, 'If you really are homosexual, you may have to learn to give and receive love that way.' At the time, I was disturbed by what he said, but not shocked, since I knew his thinking too well. Yet I had come into the Catholic Church to have my homosexuality coherently condemned. Instead, the priest said what I had never dared say to myself, and although it took four years before I took him up on it, he may have saved my life. I am eternally grateful to him.

In the short term, my entry into the Catholic Church brought me the one intense love relationship with a woman of my life. Rosemary was another Catholic convert and we fell in love and were together for three years. For two of those years, we lived together. We were very happy and I was additionally happy because my 'cover' was complete. To outsiders we were a model heterosexual couple and we very nearly married. I backed out shortly before the wedding, although in fact the collapse of my heterosexual fantasy life had begun nine months prior to that.

One afternoon when I was out shopping for the evening meal, I was followed and approached by a young man – a foreign student – who invited me back to his room for sex. I had never looked for sex before this happened yet when it did happen I was transformed on the spot. It was as intense an experience as any religious conversion that I have heard of. It was also, in superficial aspects, a sort of anti-religious conversion. The sex was very good. Luis was very sexy and good-looking; perfectly normally masculine, he was also very funny and attractively cynical. Most of all, he was utterly without guilt or fear about his sexuality. Without knowing it, he destroyed about ten false stereotypes which I had believed in to protect myself from my sexual drive.

All the negative crap which is still churned out about effeminacy, weakness and unhappiness, together with unwarranted beliefs which I seemed to have made up for myself about gay men being ugly, stupid and boring – all these went out of the window. After a lifetime of unremitting depression, I left Luis' room overjoyed to be alive and happy to be gay. I was desperately eager to make up for lost time – which I did!

Rosemary was of course heartbroken and confused. I hurt her terribly and feel deep sorrow for that, though in fairness to myself she was an unwitting victim of homophobia rather than of any wish in me to hurt her. When I first told her that I was gay she wanted us to struggle on and try to overcome it; she knew as little about homosexuality as I did. Even the Catholic chaplain encouraged us to try. But all I wanted was to experience again what I had had with Luis, so I threw myself wholeheart-edly into a time of promiscuous sexual activity. It is a period of my life which I look back on with affection and some pride and not with the shame that the church would doubtless like me to feel.

Luis, without ever knowing it, did even more for me than bring me to life. Within a day of meeting him I changed dramati-cally in a number of ways. Up to that point, I had had an exagger-ated desire to have children – a large family – and thought that life without it would not be worth living. I had a desperate need to be thought normal and conventional in other areas of my life as well as the sexual. I had a sneaking affection for the monarchy, for instance, which sat ill with my left-wing politics. All these things just disappeared, never to return. In addition, many aspects of my religious needs – for rules, traditions and the flum-mery of Tridentine liturgy – evaporated.

When I was 27, after 18 months or so of my 'sex-as-a-new-toy' phase, I met David and lived with him for the next seven years. He is still far and away my closest and dearest friend, though we haven't been lovers for many years. He is the first and the best of many good things which have come to me from the active phase of my sexual life. I loved him body and soul – soul, certainly, body perhaps to a lesser degree. In any case, after seven years I met and fell for another man – Glen – and here there was no doubt about physical attraction. Sexually, this relationship

FAITH, HOPE AND CHASTITY

was the high point of my life and for five years I lived in a tempestuous, unstable, often violent and angry, occasionally ecstatically happy love affair. It is enough to say that Glen left me to travel to wilder sexual shores than I was prepared to visit. Later he contracted Aids and died. The grief I still feel for his rejection of me and his ensuing and somehow inevitable death is intense.

Since Glen's death I have had no great love affair and for many years no sexual activity of any kind. My heart is full with Glen and, in a more enduring way, with David. Also, I am growing old. When I was young, I vowed never to be a desperate older man hopefully but futilely going around gay pubs and discos. I have never been a confident cruiser, and with age what confidence I did have has gone. In any case, my sexual drive is no longer overpoweringly insistent. Furthermore, to have a varied and extensive sexual history to look back on seems to take away any great need to add to it. Sexual desire is still there, of course, but, even though it is not now expressed, it is more of an enhancement to my life than a torment. I love to see a good-looking man in the street; I no longer have a pressing urge to have him.

In the beginning I clung to the Catholic faith by my fingertips, not infrequently turning up to Sunday Mass from the bed of a Saturday night pick-up. There was always a greater depth to my belief than the flummery of Catholic ritual, always an excitement about the person of Jesus Christ and the things he said and did, always a perception of the essential futility and absurdity of an empty, God-less universe. My passionate identification with the underdog and with those who suffer has remained intense and constant through all the fluctuations of my life. I have always had a deep desire to live and to preach, by word and example, the gospel of Jesus Christ as I understand and feel it; I have at depth always wanted to be a priest.

After 15 years of work – the time of David and Glen – and much prayer, thought and discussion, I entered seminary to train for the Catholic priesthood. After years of living on my own I enjoyed my seminary time – the study, the worship and the close company of others. I relapsed while I was there into a rather irritating phase of neo-conservatism, possibly in reaction to the prevailing and rather uncritical liberalism of the seminary and possibly for reasons more connected with my own ineradicable psyche. Whatever it was, that conservatism was dispelled when I began my pastoral work as a deacon. So many of the concerns and priorities of the conservatives, and I include the Pope, are utterly, embarrassingly irrelevant to the ways in which people actually live their lives. It is not the case that those concerns and priorities challenge the ways of the world in any prophetic way; they are actually enclosed in a self-contained universe which rarely touches the world that most people inhabit. Even if the great majority of people on the council estate where I began my pastoral work did feel an attachment to the Church, they would also feel themselves cut off from it and excluded by the hierarchy because of some sexual or marital or procreational infringement.

I am very happy working as a celibate Catholic priest. In some ways this is the happiest period of my life so far – and my life has been far from uniformly miserable. Although in the poor inner-city parish where I work fewer than ten per cent of nominal Catholics attend Mass, and most of those are very old, I find that people are incredibly responsive to and grateful for the ministry of the Church. But that ministry has to be showing them and telling them the good news of Jesus Christ which says that no matter what marital or other tangle they may find themselves in, no matter what they have done or have failed to do, they are of infinite worth, deserving of care and respect, and their lives have great significance and value, especially if they are outcast or deemed of no account in the eyes of the world.

I find most of the emanations from Rome merely an embarrassment and a hindrance. I'll use the example of homosexuality since I know about that inside and out, although what I say can easily be applied to the unmarried, the married who are fertile and to those whose current relationships cannot be recognized by the Church – indeed, to all the sexually active, which is most of the human race.

Homosexuality is a condition, usually irreversible, over which the individual has no say. The writers of the Old Testament didn't know this. St Paul clearly didn't know this. Indeed, the concept of homosexuality as a condition rather than a deliberate, freely chosen and perverse action was not isolated until the nineteenth century. For a homosexual, as for any other man or woman, the

FAITH, HOPE AND CHASTITY

desire for sex is powerfully and mysteriously connected with the deepest levels of the human psyche – most notably the capacity to fall in love and for that love, sexually expressed, to mature into intimacy. Great damage – moral damage – can be done to a person taught to despise their sexuality, because it is their sexuality which lies at the heart of their ability to love.

Yet the Church demands that homosexuals think of themselves as disordered and defective. It labels as grave sin – for homosexuals – any genital expression of that insistent sexual desire which is present at the centre of every woman and man. I think that the *Letter to Bishops on the Pastoral Care of Homosexual People* which the Congregation for the Doctrine of the Faith – the Inquisition – sent to every bishop in the world is one of the most evil documents of this century. Change the word 'homosexual' to 'Jew' and Julius Streicher would not have been ashamed of it. It seems to hint that homosexuals may be responsible for their condition, in that if they practise it they will become more fixed in it. It quite clearly states that although queer-bashing is to be deprecated, homosexuals themselves bear some of the blame for the phenomenon by having the temerity to object to their own oppression. The document assumes that bishops will fight to retain the laws which criminalize homosexuals in areas where they are outlawed and it insists that any Catholic group which even questions the law and practice of the Church on these matters should be banned from church premises. No bishop has ever repudiated this document. No bishop has ever stated that it is pre-scientific, tendentious, uncharitable and unfair. Instead the bishops, some of them at least, do their utmost to say nice-sounding things about homosexuals while of course forbidding under pain of sin any sexual act. They try to be friendly to homosexuals and at the same time obedient to the Vatican; the posture which they must therefore adopt is seen as either ridiculous or disingenuous.

In the meantime the world, which with the approval of the Church used to hang homosexuals, has come increasingly to accept us. For the young, tolerance of gay people is almost the touchstone of enlightenment – any youth programme on late night television gives evidence of that. Even the leaders of the Conservative Party have recently challenged the homophobia which used to be the bedrock of their traditional values. Only the most ignorant sections of society – the ones where racism still flourishes unchecked – still think it clever to laugh at or beat up queers or to condemn people for a condition which, of itself, causes no harm and over which an individual has no control. The Catholic Church is the only institution of any standing which still tries to make homosexuals feel guilty and small and which still encourages morally censorious attitudes towards them amongst its members. This, the Church of Christ, who out-raged the respectable of his time by befriending and respecting tax-collectors, prostitutes, widows and lepers.

There are ways of shedding the gospel light on human sexual-ity that don't manage to alienate 98 per cent of the human race. There are ways of highlighting the awesome, noble, yet reward-ing and delightful calling of marriage and children without putting down the infertile, the gay, the single and those who choose not to have children. But the Church is trapped by its past and seems unable to say that it has got something wrong. It has though. Toleration of slavery, condemnation of usury, the asser-tion that all those not subject to the Roman Pontiff were certainly damned and that Galileo challenged the Church's authori-tative interpretation of the Book of Judges are just a few exam-ples of where the Church has got things horribly wrong.

It has been shrewdly said that sex is the Church's Galileo crisis of the twentieth century. I believe this is accurate and not merely clever. If I were to feel bound by the Vatican line in all things, pastorally I would be in an impossible position. Last year, the bishop gave each priest a document from Rome – *Vade Mecum* – on how to guide married couples who use contraception when they mention this matter in confession. It was sent to every priest in the world. Quite apart from its content, which I thought daft, no one in Rome seems to realize that almost nobody – in England at least – comes to confession, especially not people who are sexually active. In the unlikely event of a sexually active married man or woman coming to confession, contraception would simply not be mentioned. On which planet do these Vati-can prelates live?

In the parish where I work, relatively few people's lives con-form to the approved Vatican model for licit sex; this means that if I hold to the Vatican line, a high proportion of those who attend Mass cannot receive Holy Communion. That causes scandal. Even the most respectable members of the congregation are scandalized when their neighbours, possibly because of some painful marriage breakdown of years before, are barred from receiving Holy Communion. Yet Rome seems to think that the scandal would be caused the other way round if such people were allowed to receive the sacraments.

I think the Church's teaching on sex is the main cause of the collapse of the Catholic Church in England. I may be wrong but surely no one can doubt that the Church's sexual teaching, together with the uncaring and negative attitudes of many who propound it, has at least contributed to the marginalization of the Catholic faith in this country. All of which is tragically unnecessary. For Christianity is not a taboo religion. Christ came, at least in part, to liberate us from that, from the notion that certain acts or gestures or places are displeasing to God in themselves. What is in the heart is what counts – no action can be labelled sinful per se. Sin is that which causes harm, directly and demonstrably, to ourselves or more importantly, to others. What harm is done if two men who love each other and who are gay express that love sexually? And if no obvious harm is caused, how can it be gravely sinful?

My scorn of the Church's teaching on sexual morality may suggest that I am in the wrong outfit, that I have no place in the Catholic Church, particularly not as a priest. Yet my anger comes from love and not from rejection. I am by no means alone in what I think even if my personal involvement makes me more passionate in my frustration than many others might be. While the Church remains incapable of absorbing and building a new understanding as it formulates its attitudes to human sexuality, the world is completely at sea. The world needs to hear about the gospel proclamation of fidelity, the importance of intimacy and about the awesome responsibility of bringing life into being and providing the opportunity for it to flourish.

There are some wonderful, distinctively Christian attitudes to human sexuality that the world desperately needs to hear. Alas, no one is listening; most people think of the Catholic Church, if they think of it at all, as a negative, judgemental, puritanical institution which burdens practically everyone with guilt. 'Beware the Scribes and Pharisees. For they tie up heavy burdens, hard to bear, and lay them on the shoulders of others; but they themselves are unwilling to lift a finger to move them' (Matthew 23:4).

8. Cardinal Thomas Winning

Cardinal Thomas Winning, Archbishop of Glasgow,
was born in Lanarkshire, Scotland in 1925

Thomas Winning is the Jimmy Knapp of the Catholic Church –
raw, working class and not a little feared. Known as he is for his
outspoken views, I expected the Cardinal to be blunt and intimi-
dating. I could not have been more wrong. Such was my surprise
on meeting him that I found myself temporarily speechless. He
was shorter than I had expected but also much younger-looking
than his 72 years would suggest. After an agonizing pause in
which the proper address for a Cardinal entirely escaped me, I
managed to utter, 'Hello, Father.'
Unlike many of his contemporaries, Cardinal Winning has
been blessed with a rock-like faith. The dark world of doubts and
spiritual crises is not one with which he has grappled; in his own
words, faith has been 'plain sailing'. The outcome is a person
who is sure of his religion and its teachings – too sure perhaps.
While plainly a man of the people, the Cardinal lacks the sub-
tlety and imagination of one who has experienced life's greyer
areas at first hand. Having said that, his approach to me person-
ally was singularly pastoral. I was clearly a human being to him
and not just another interviewer. He worried about my cough,
he refilled my tea cup, he chatted. Whatever his personal limita-
tions, the Cardinal undoubtedly makes up for them in kindness.

I don't ever see myself as Pope. I was in Rome recently for what's
called the 'ad limina' visit when bishops report to the Holy Father
every five years on the progress of their dioceses. I was visiting

the Sistine Chapel when a steward invited me over to see what he called the 'Camera del Pianto', or 'Room of Tears'. I found myself in this little room leading off the back of the Chapel with stairs running up one side and down the other, almost a kind of transit camp. 'What's this?' I said. 'And why is it called the Room of Tears?' The steward explained, 'This is where they bring the Pope after he's been elected. It's in here that he tries on the three cassocks to see which one fits him. That's why they call it the "Room of Tears".' And I thought, 'My God, poor guys. If these walls could only speak.' So, no, I wouldn't have it, I wouldn't want to be Pope.

Round about the age of 13 I knew I wanted to be a priest. I felt rather embarrassed about it because boys are supposed to be boys – being religious was for softies. Our parish was a very vibrant, community-minded parish in which more or less the same four priests served six or seven thousand people. I was recruited into the choir at about the age of ten although really I would have preferred to be an altar boy – being in the sanctuary meant you were close to the action. There were 20 or 30 altar boys and in the end I was invited to join them. The priest who asked me remained a parish priest while I went on to become Archbishop. Having been his altar boy, when he'd say, 'Let me see your fingers, let me see that your nails are clean', I always marvelled at the way he respected me. He would call me by my first name but he'd a great respect. I thought, 'My goodness, here's my priest and now I'm his Archbishop.' It was a very touching relationship. He was very good.

I remember my first parish. The parish priest left after a week for a month's holiday and I was a rookie in the place. I remember running down through the football field on my first 'sick call' to attend someone in danger of death. I'd only ever seen one dead body in my life and I always dreaded being called out to a street accident or something like that. You can't imagine what sick calls are like until you get one. They made me see that there are an infinite variety of ways in which people die. I also remember starting a football team in the parish and being beaten 10–1 the first time we played. During the game one of the team got a bad gash in his knee – one minute I was studying it and cleaning it up, the next minute I was having a cup of tea in somebody's house. I was 24 and I'd fainted at the sight of his blood.

I remember a kid – a wee fellow – asking me in a school one day, 'Why don't priests get married?' I said, 'Son, if I had ever married, my wife would have divorced me years ago because I'm never in the house, I'm never at home.' How could I, as a priest, bring up children? In addition, of course, I could not do one third of what I do now if I had dependents like a wife and children. One of the difficulties today is that we want instant this and instant that, and lifelong commitments are no longer fashionable. It's the same with the priesthood. My heart's broken when young men come to me, often after they've been some 13-odd years on the road, and say, 'My future is not in the ministry.' It makes me wonder what's happening because they're not *all* bad, they haven't all had a kind of dreadful change of heart.

I remember somebody in the Holy Office who dealt with dispensations for priests wanting to leave the priesthood. Having spent years reading their stories and studying their cases, he said there wasn't one who didn't have a crisis of faith somewhere along the line. I suspect that some of the young men stop saying their breviary, it just gets pitched into a corner. They are more or less obliged to celebrate Mass publicly but their heart eventually isn't in it. Their lifestyle, while not being excessively worldly, helps them to lose their interest for anything spiritual. Then there comes a point when they begin to think of themselves as hypocrites because they're playing an external role but inside they just don't mean it, and then they reach a point when they can no longer cope with this. So they decide to leave. Hence the reason for usually saying, 'What a relief!' It's relief from no longer acting out a part they can't believe in. But why do they no longer believe in it? I think it's because they didn't work at it.

Celibacy doesn't affect the shortage of priests. The Church of Scotland is short of ministers and yet they accept women; the Anglicans are the same. There are several reasons for the lack of vocations. People have fewer children now. Whereas before there were four or five in a family, now there's only one or two so we've fewer to choose from. Sometimes I go up to Glasgow University or to a Catholic secondary school and talk to 100 people in the sixth form and say, 'If I had five of you, you'd solve my problems.' But they don't come.

Celibacy's been hard for me, yes – I'm a normal person, but it's not something that's kept preying on my mind; it's not the biggest thing in my life. Even so, when I see people caring for each other, or when I see people in love, I do find something very attractive in it. Trying to keep close to my prayer life and being involved with other people has helped me over that kind of difficulty so that I've never really felt lonely – never – or only now and again. I've kept close to my own family, but also the people here in Glasgow are so appreciative of anything I do for them that they more than make up for the lack of a wife and family to me. They're like my own flesh and blood.

One problem that's going to aggravate the issue of celibacy is the number of married clergy coming over from the Anglican Church. Priests are going to say, 'Why should this inequality exist? So-and-so can have his wife and children and celebrate Mass and be a Catholic priest in every sense of the word, so why not me?' I think it's going to raise questions amongst the clergy – mainly in England since it hardly affects us in Scotland. I've always been very clear that celibacy is a discipline of the Church. I would find it difficult to justify changing it at this time when society's so mad about sex. The tabloids would probably be the first to condemn us for it – they usually try to reach the moral high ground before anyone else. I think it was Chesterton who said something about not being able to win with celibacy: if you have it, they make a fool of you, and if you break it, they make a fool of you.

The other challenge for the Church is to be prophetic, and by prophetic I mean championing the qualities of the Kingdom of God and denouncing situations where the opposites are true. I think that people are encouraged when someone does that. I was very moved by the reaction I got when I made an offer to help young women facing a crisis pregnancy. So many people wrote to me from all over Britain, many enclosing cheques. That offer seemed to touch a nerve; in the first nine months it helped save around 50 babies' lives. If I had helped just one woman keep her baby I would have been happy. But 50? It's great. I think the response to that offer revealed a great unease in Britain about an abortion law which has killed five million people in 30 years. No one could have foreseen that it would be as bad as this.

FAITH, HOPE AND CHASTITY

I don't always expect other bishops to support me. On one occasion I took Prince Charles to task about the Act of Succession which bars Catholics from succeeding to the throne. He had spoken about dogmas, you know, right and wrong, good and bad. He'd made a very simplistic statement about Prince Michael having to go to Austria to get married because his bride, Princess Michael, was a Catholic and her first union was being annulled. The Prince was actually speaking at a Salvation Army function that day, and of course in the Salvation Army if you don't marry a person in the citadel you've got to get out of it, so really he chose the wrong location. But I didn't say that at the time. I simply said, 'What about the Act of Succession? You're passing judgements on the Catholic laws of marriage, what about your law?' Our media officer at the time said, 'You know, I just want to warn you that you're the first to say this. Tomorrow, or this afternoon, other bishops will come in with other statements and yours will go to the bottom of the pile.' Well, nobody said anything. They were all under their beds in the middle of summer. It reverberated for about three weeks until in the end I didn't want to open a newspaper. Even *The Times* had letters about it. 'God save the Prince of Wales,' wrote Lord Hailsham and I thought, 'Well, there's a lesson for you.' Nobody, but nobody among my colleagues came and gave me a sympathetic shake of the hand or a sympathetic word. Some of them did it months later, but none of them did it at the time and I felt more lonely than I've ever been – so much so that when Cardinal O'Fiaich made a statement about the Maze prison and Lord Rollinson gave him hell for it, I wrote to the Cardinal and said, 'I know how lonely it is when you've said something and people jump on your back.' Some months later one of Paul VI's closest collaborators told me the Holy Father had welcomed my comment.

Pope John Paul II is a man with tremendous charisma – a very saintly man. Two experiences convinced me of that. One was when Derek Worlock and I went out to Rome to see if we could persuade him to continue with his plan to visit Britain. This was during the Falklands War and he was getting pressure from the South Americans not to come. We were at lunch when his valet brought in a message which he put down on the table. The Pope read the message and then looked up and continued to talk.

When we got out we discovered the content of the message: Britain had just invaded the Falklands. The Pope had a perfect trust in God and the guidance of the Holy Spirit. 'The Church must rise above politics,' he said, 'and do what we have to do.' I felt the gift of the Spirit was so much in him. I'm sure he doesn't take blood pressure tablets or anything like that. He's got a tranquillity which comes from living in the Spirit.

And then there was the shooting incident and the aftermath of that which was quite extraordinary. The bullet went into his stomach and then travelled downwards when by rights it should have gone into his stomach and up. If it had done that, it would have gone right to his heart and killed him. Bishop Magee was the Pope's secretary at the time and I remember asking him whether the Pope ever mentioned being shot. Bishop Magee said, 'Well, he once said he thought it was a bomb but that when he felt the pain inside and saw the blood, he realized he'd been shot.' Apparently it struck the Pope that maybe Our Lady was asking him to shed his blood for the Church. Bishop Magee said that when the Pope realized that might well be the case, he knew he wasn't going to die because he felt the Fatima prophecy was coming true. Our Lady appeared to peasant children in Fatima in Portugal in 1917 and said, 'The Holy Father will have much to suffer.' Apparently he reasoned that if he was to suffer, he had to live. That's good thinking when you're lying at the bottom of a truck bleeding to death. The Pope has recalled many times that he was shot on the anniversary of the apparitions and he credits his survival to Our Lady's protection.

The love and affection that people have shown me is the greatest reward of priesthood. Being a bishop or a cardinal has never gone to my head. I like people, I've got a kind of gut feeling for people, and they know that. Even if you're just a simple priest in a parish – and that's all I ever aspired to be – I think they appreciate it. I used to have older priests with me as assistants who couldn't wait for the day when they'd become parish priests, but I didn't care tuppence about that. Without a doubt I could die today and not regret one bit, one moment of being a priest. It's not a priest's education really that makes him special, it's his closeness to God; the Grace of God does it. I've never suffered a great deal – I think I've been very fortunate. I've often thought that either I was too stupid to have any doubts or that it was just plain sailing for me, but I've never had any real doubts. I might have regrets about what I've done in a sinful sense, but I wouldn't have any regrets about serving the people of Scotland – none. It's been a great gift, a great privilege. Glasgow folk are special, they're very warm-hearted and good-humoured – a bit like the Liverpudlians. Down south they sometimes give the impression of being a bit stuck up!

9. Father Jim O'Keefe

Fr Jim O'Keefe was born in County Durham in 1948

Fr Jim O'Keefe's thick County Durham accent somehow accentuates the warmth and down-to-earthness of his personality. Known by the Catholic hierarchy as a good priest – approachable, bright, useful – he's recently been made rector of Ushaw Seminary in the north-east of England and is currently engaged in modernizing those training courses which prepare seminarians for the life of celibacy which awaits them. Fr Jim has also been pivotal in drawing up the Catholic Church's various policy documents which address the problem of child abuse amongst the clergy.[1] His chapter is dedicated to this issue since, as a counsellor, Fr Jim has real insight into the needs of people who have been abused. Brought up in a conventional working class Catholic family, Father O'Keefe is essentially a private man who has achieved a great deal in his ministry. Perhaps he is one of those who subconsciously joined the priesthood in order to avoid the demands of fully fledged relationships. If he is, it has been to the Church's gain.

---

[1] In 1990 the Social Welfare Committee of the Bishops' Conference published *Sex Abuse and the Catholic Church*. One of its nine recommendations was that there should be national guidelines for the Catholic Church. These guidelines were set out in the *Budd Report* which in turn recommended further work on the pastoral care of abused children, communities and colleagues. This became *Healing the Wound*, which included recommendations for further work concerning the care of abusers.

FAITH, HOPE AND CHASTITY

Much of my work in recent years has been to do with sexual abuse and the Church. It started eight years ago when I was the administrator of a diocesan social welfare agency and it emerged that the deputy headmaster of a Catholic school in our diocese had been systematically abusing children for over 20 years. It was a small school in a very traditional Catholic area on the coast of County Durham. Mothers who had themselves been abused as children sent their own children to the same school who were then also abused, because in such a small, tight community it would have been an even bigger scandal if they had sent their kids to the local state school and not to the Catholic school.

The social services department in County Durham just couldn't comprehend this and asked us, as a Catholic agency, to work on behalf of the local authority. I was employing 15 social workers at the time and that was my first experience of the issues around abuse – the effect on the teachers, the children, the families and on the community as a whole, because this man was a well-respected person in the parish.

At the beginning of my work with sex abuse victims it was very frightening because I didn't know what the limits or the rules were. I didn't know whether you had to be very strict with people or very non-directive. I didn't know the language; I didn't understand that when a person has been abused, their sense of self and of trust is totally destroyed. It's to do with the total infringement of one's personal space, so that if a child is sexually abused they have no sense of their own limits. Some children close right in and become very isolated and sexually dysfunctional; others do the opposite and become totally promiscuous because they have no sense of where the limits and the boundaries are. It reminds me of a six-year-old lad in foster care who was placed with a family up here. He went to a swimming pool with his foster father and in the changing room he said, 'If you give that man money he'll do it to me.' This boy was so sexually aware that he could sense any kind of vulnerability or deviance in adults.

In some ways it's no worse whether the abuser is a priest or your grandfather or your brother. Whoever abuses you, it's still abuse. And yet because of the symbolic leadership role of the priest, the fact remains that he's meant to be better than the rest of us. I know that people whose marriages have been witnessed by a priest who has abused children worry about their marriages being valid – whether they're proper and right.

I think some people who have been abused find the whole imagery of the Church immensely difficult. I'm generalizing now, not because I don't have ideas but because I'm taking a voice from someone when everybody else has been taking from them as well. But some people do find it enormously difficult to cope with the notion of God as Father because their own father abused them. They also can't cope with what they see as men dressing up as women; they see that as deviant. Concelebration is difficult because they simply see a group of men who in their eyes are potential abusers.

One of the effects on whole communities is that suddenly there's a 'sexualization' of the priest. Until then it never occurred to people to imagine a priest being involved in sexual activity. It's not fair to use the same word but whole communities do become *traumatized* and anyone fragile loses their sense of control. So if they're prone to depression, for example, they become *more* depressed, or if they're agoraphobic, they become more agoraphobic. Their difficulty, whatever it may be, is increased.

A parish can become named as an 'abused' parish and people stop going to Mass there from other parishes in case they get contaminated. There's a parish in Durham where this is actually happening at the moment. The priest is in prison – he comes to court fairly soon – and folk are frightened to come together in groups. Yet the care of the elderly and the housebound still has to go on.

The issue of abuse affects the Church deeply in a whole range of areas. It's fundamentally about power, because sexual abuse is as much about the abuse of power as about the sexuality of a vulnerable person. It says something about the lifestyle of clergy and the need to be more open to our own personal and sexual development. Priests must be much more professionally aware so that, for example, we don't go off with kids on our own, because the fact is, it's healthier to have adults and youngsters mixed together. We don't have kids overnight in the presbytery when we're alone, not just because it doesn't look good, but because it can be threatening – it's the wrong sign.

FAITH, HOPE AND CHASTITY

People can come through this kind of experience but they may need frequent opportunities to tell their story; other people just need to tell it once or twice. When people are feeling confused or distraught, they need someone to incarnate the love of God. They need someone to make that love real. 'Don't tell me about God,' they say. 'If I'm in a mess, just sit with me and be in a mess with me so that I know it's OK to be in a mess.' People can go from being 'abused' to being 'survivors' to being 'thrivers' but the danger is always of being flipped back into the survival mode or into the distraught mode. So healing is unquestionably possible but the scars will always be there.

If an accusation is made against a priest, the question then is, how do we justly, respectfully and honourably respond to that accusation? It might just be a cry for attention – it may never have happened. There are cases – very few – where there have been accusations which are false. In the interests of the Church, the priest and the individual making the accusation, it *must* be looked at thoroughly.

If the accusation is proven to be false, it demands a lot of openness and compassion in relation to the priest because some would think there's no smoke without fire. It takes a lot of courage on the priest's behalf to get stuck back into his ministry. And in relation to the person who's fabricating the story, there's obviously a need for genuine help. The difficulty occurs when there's an accusation which may have something in it but not enough evidence to prove it. Then we have difficulties and I think all we can do is comply fully with any local authority or statutory inquiry. And if the Church isn't satisfied with that, it must go forward with its own inquiry.

My work on the issues around abuse has made me acutely aware of the way people in the Church walk, talk, dress – all those non-verbal ways in which power can be exercised. I used to feel quite threatened by the way people who had been abused would tell me that I didn't understand and that I wasn't listening, when I thought I was listening *dead hard* and was being dead compassionate. And yet I was using language and symbols that they found offensive, and I found that very painful. I'll never fully understand what abuse is like – never – but I'm closer to understanding it than when I began. The danger is that we're so frightened of other people's pain that we won't go near it. Or, we become so absorbed by it that we simply increase by one the number of fragile people in the world.

The word 'forgiveness' is too quick. Forgiveness is a lifelong task and all we can initially ask from people who have been abused is that they should not want to wipe out the person who abused them. Abusers are around; they're in our community. Any one of us is capable of abusing power and doing things that are shameful. We're in a culture where, thankfully, the child and the integrity of the child is paramount and any destroying of that is a tragic event. We've only just begun to ask the question, 'Can abusers get to the stage of being able to control it?' A whole range of people sexually abuse others. There's a difference between a child abuser and a paedophile and it's important that our knowledge increases. So, for example, there are paedophiles who are regressive. In other words, under certain circumstances – under strain – they regress into a stage of arrested development in which they abuse children. Is that more controllable than someone who's permanently in that state?

If we're going to be serious about child abuse as a Church, we have to have people who know these distinctions and know about therapy and control. My experience is limited, but people who are Schedule 1 offenders – in other words, they've been through the courts and prison – find it *enormously* difficult to consider going back into any worshipping community or any community at all. Our resources don't go into the people who are at the bottom of the pile. But maybe we've got to grow up and become more compassionate towards them. Because at the moment if you're a paedophile you've got no chance really, certainly not within the prison community and if it's known outside, not much chance there either. We're not good at acknowledging that people who do *very* wrong things are also capable of doing very good things. We're not *that* good at appreciating that people who do very good things can also do wrong things. We want every-thing to be clear and black and white. We want our public leaders to be shining and they're not, they're frail and weak. Part of the problem is how we cope with evil in our midst. It's as though we stuff these people with all the confusions and shame we have about sexuality because this is a particularly heinous crime, and then we make them suffer for it. As a community we look for scapegoats. We like to be able to put all our collective evil into people and then push them off into the desert or behind a brick wall – castrate them and hang them. I think we'll never really understand forgiveness until we explore all this and become more mature about it.

I remember one time when I was a student here at Ushaw. I was about 20 and it was the feast of Corpus Christi. We had the big procession with the president carrying the monstrance with the host in it and I remember clearly thinking, 'I don't know whether I believe in any of this or not – transubstantiation, the Eucharist – all of it.' Our teachers were very good at asking us what the Eucharist meant in order that we should go away and write essays on it. But what it meant to us *personally* was never on the agenda.

At the time I didn't really do anything; I was scared of saying I couldn't cope. If you come from the north-east of England, you have that sort of background, it's almost a subcultural thing. So I didn't do anything – I just hung in with it for a bit and the intense fear eventually drifted away. Now when I look back on those doubts and fears as a 20-year-old, I see them as a kind of questioning. I'm no longer scared about the intellectual questions of whether the bread and wine are the body and blood of Jesus – I'll just hang in with that and try to make sense of it. But when it comes to living out the Eucharist – ah – that's when I begin to doubt and to think to myself, 'God, have I got the bottle for this?' I mean, Kierkegaard said that if you take Christianity neat it'll kill you and I think he was right.

Living out the Eucharist means looking at what we do – the decisions we make, the things we put in place – through the perspective of folk who are powerless. Living it out means taking brokenness as the centre and struggling towards oneness and unity and reconciling all things. I have a particular picture in my room called *The Descent Into Hell*. It's got Adam and Eve in it with the broken cross in the middle and it's about bringing together opposites. For me, the Eucharist is about interpreting the plight of those who are powerless in language that those *with* power might appreciate. It's about standing in the middle somewhere between rich and poor and saying, 'Be compassionate, as your heavenly Father is compassionate.' I think that's what we're called to do.

10. Bishop Vincent Nichols

Bishop Vincent Nichols, Bishop in North London,
was born in Crosby, Liverpool in 1945

Bishop Vincent Nichols, one of the men most tipped to succeed
Cardinal Hume as Archbishop of Westminster, is, at 54, a com-
paratively young bishop. Raised in a suburb of Liverpool by
parents who were both teachers, his rise through the ranks of the
Catholic hierarchy has been meteoric. Gifted as a communicator,
especially with the media, and noted for his brilliant manage-
ment skills, Bishop Nichols is a thoroughly professional operator
who would certainly provide thoughtful and serious leadership
for the four million Catholics of England and Wales.

Armed with ease and a polite goodwill, Bishop Nichols was a
hard nut to crack. He spoke cautiously about his feelings, especially
negative ones, and revealed very little of his inner self. The most
important thread which runs throughout this chapter concerns
the bishop's relationship with his father, a man who trained for the
priesthood but was rejected by his seminary after several years of
study. People often think that it is the mother who hands down her
own vocation to her son. In the case of Bishop Nichols, his voca-
tion, if not inherited from his father, was most certainly influenced
by him. When I asked the bishop about this possible link, he simply
smiled and said, 'I don't know. It is God's Providence.'

One of the important features of the Catholic priesthood is that
we live where we work. We're shopping in the same shops, we're
eating the same kind of food, we're there alongside people. That
was very strong in south Liverpool and now that I'm a bishop,

I miss that sense of continuity. When you work in a parish you really do accompany people, and they accompany you, and there's a terrific bond of support, both ways. But for that you need time and you need stability. Now as a bishop I just move around 50 parishes and there's no chance of accompanying people in that immediate way any more. Now it's much more distant, it's much more symbolic.

I grew up in Crosby, a suburb on the north side of Liverpool just beyond the docks. It was known as 'Debtors' Retreat' because people who had failed in Liverpool moved out of their bigger houses to live in smaller ones in Crosby. It has always had a strong Catholic tradition; three bishops have been ordained from the parish I grew up in.

Ours was a house in which there was a great practice of the faith, so we would pray together as a family, but there was also a great intellectual interest in the faith. Even as children we would be aware of my parents and their friends gathering, say, on a Sunday night and having terrific discussions about every aspect of faith – and not just compliant discussions but vigorous ones. As I grew older I had energetic arguments with my father on just about every aspect of faith. It was also a household in which priests were around – priests in the parish, a cousin of my mother's who was a priest, his friends – they were often to be found having a cup of tea in the kitchen. So there was a great ease of living a Catholic life, but it was also an exciting thing to do – it was a real and challenging thing to do.

I went to a secondary school run by the Christian Brothers. It was vigorous. There was lots of academic push and a strong method of discipline. There was also corporal punishment but it was not sadistic; it was just the accepted style of the day and I have no complaints at all about the way I was treated there. I was punished for things like poor homework or misbehaviour in class. We were given other opportunities as well. The one that had a big influence on me was the school orchestra. I learnt to play the French horn and that has enriched my priesthood and life. It opened up the whole world of orchestral music because, just as cricket makes sense if you've played it and if you haven't played it, it's rather difficult to understand, so too with orchestral music. It's much more exciting if you've been part of an orchestra. It also taught me a lot about teamwork and corporate effort.

I started to become aware of the nagging presence of a vocation within me at around the age of 15. I remember going to speak to one of the priests in the parish and saying to him, 'You know, I think maybe I ought to be a priest,' and I always remember his reply. He said to me, 'The first thing I want you to know is that it is not a sin to refuse a vocation.' So right from the very word go, he was taking away any pressure that I might feel. And I also remember that in the course of that evening the younger curate came into the room and – because I was upstairs in the presbytery which was very unusual – this other priest looked at me and said, 'What on earth are you doing here?' When he heard that I was talking about whether or not I had a vocation he said – teasingly – 'Goodness me, don't get involved in this, it's *awful*.' Again it was exactly the right response.

I assumed that if I was taken on I would go to the diocesan seminary at Upholland. In fact, my father had spent quite a number of years at the seminary and had then been eased out – he'd been thrown out really. I think he was too much of an individualist; I think that was the top and bottom of it. He never really gave me a fuller explanation and I never asked.

In those days, bright students were kept back to act as teachers to the junior seminarian pupils and my father did this for three years, after which he went to Freiburg to do a year's theology. But then when he came back, somehow the decision was made that he wasn't really suited to the priesthood. It meant, however, that he taught a good number of the diocesan priests in Liverpool, so they all knew my father. My father never said a single word, neither for nor against, my sense of vocation. He just didn't say anything. I think he had been very hurt by his own rejection because he wanted to be a priest, but he never passed on an iota of that hurt to me. I only found out most of those things after he died. But the priests of the diocese had appreciated him enormously and used to come to me and say, 'Look, I hope you understand what your dad did and what a difference he made to our lives as youngsters in the seminary. He had a great sense of fun and he used to liven things up for us.'

Going to Rome was a bit of a shock. I remember going to see Cardinal Heenan, or Archbishop Heenan as he was then, and not even knowing that a seminary existed in Rome. At the end of my interview Archbishop Heenan said, 'Well, I'm going to send you to the English College in Rome.' I had to wait until he left the room before saying, 'What's that? When do I go?' and, 'When do I come home?' I learned that once you went to Rome you didn't come home for three years. My parents were remarkable. They said, 'No, if that's what the bishop wants, that's what we do.' They were very clear about the way the Church works and I suppose that's still very deep within me.

I remember thinking, 'This is appalling. I'm not going to go home for Christmas.' All I got by way of compensation was a weekly copy of the *Liverpool Football Echo* every Tuesday to tell me how the teams had got on, but the college was good in a number of ways. I found that living in Rome gave me a very immediate sense of the universality of the Church. Also, I was there during four of the years of the Second Vatican Council. It meant that every evening during supper, while the Council was in session from about October to December, we would be read press reports of the speeches made that day. I followed the work of the Second Vatican Council very closely, and that was a great privilege.

The first big challenge I had to face was as chaplain to a sixth form college in Liverpool. I remember to this day arriving at the sixth form college at precisely the wrong moment – twenty to four – when 600 teenagers were coming out and I was trying to go in. It was a most appalling moment. Suddenly I thought, 'My goodness me, how am I supposed to relate to this mass of teenage boys and girls? How on earth am I going to do this?' I decided to set myself the fairly low objective of hoping that these youngsters, after two years at the sixth form college, would go away with the strong impression that a priest was somebody they could approach and talk to. That was enough. And I think because I set off to do that and to work hard at the human relations, we got on quite well and I'm still in touch with quite a lot of them. I enjoyed the years in the sixth form college very much indeed.

But my years as a priest in the parish in Toxteth, south Liverpool, still rank as the happiest days of my priesthood. It's an area of some deprivation and real social problems but there's a great immediacy of relationships between priest and people. The churches were not full. In fact we had a huge church – St Anne's – which had been a Benedictine church, and I don't suppose more than 300 people came in on a Sunday. So it meant we had to ask ourselves, 'What are we doing here? What are we trying to do?' And with the priests in the deanery we used to have some really good discussions about how the Church should operate in a situation like this. It was also a lot of fun. We set up an adult education centre to give people an opportunity to study English again, or perhaps to pass an O level exam which they never managed at school – or get into art. We also had a little orchestra there. We did all sorts of things to enrich people whose lives were, by force of circumstances, rather impoverished.

As a bishop the biggest thing I have to deal with is the sense of being powerful that the role of bishop has gathered to it, whereas in fact there are lots and lots of things that I can do very little about. For example, I cannot produce ideal priests for every parish at the drop of a hat. We have the priests that God has given us, and they're all shapes and sizes. It often means I cannot match the needs of a parish with the priest who might be the blueprint for that place. That's a fact and there's nothing I can do about that. I'm often asked to settle arguments and disputes and to arbitrate when people fall out. People get upset about something the parish priest has said or vice versa, or there are rows between different groups in parishes – those sorts of things. But I cannot change human nature and that's one of the limitations of the job; sometimes I'm attributed with capacities that in fact are unreal.

I move too rapidly across a whole range of subjects and issues, without ever being able to get into them as much as I would like. Today, for example, is made up of a series of interviews with people coming to talk to me about a whole range of things, things that bother them. One person's been talking about the initiative they have in a youth centre and how that might be developed. Another person who helps me with ecumenical things has been in so we reviewed some of those. Now there's this. Next there will be a priest who's asked to see me – I don't know why yet but it could be anything. Then there's a lady who wants to come and talk about her frustrations with the marriage tribunal. Then there's the Sister who acts on my behalf in relation to all the religious in the area – about 300 plus – and on we go. So the issues are as wide and as varied as the life of the local Church.

Somebody said to me yesterday, 'What I would really like is to get a computer terminal on your desk, because that would make it so much easier when we have to draft and redraft things.' I said with a vehemence that surprised me, 'I don't want one.' I was thinking about that last night and I thought, 'No, my business is not really to do with paper. My business is to do with people.' A computer terminal on the desk gives precisely the wrong signal. If the papers take a little longer to deal with, that's fine by me, because what is far more important is to have time for people and to respond to them as people in a relationship rather than as a problem. I suppose in some ways the shift from being General Secretary of the Bishops' Conference to being an auxiliary bishop has been very good for me, because it's backed me out of many of those administrative things and given me much more scope to be a part – a rather unusual part – of the life of parishes and therefore of people. The trick to being an ecclesiastical administrator is to try and remember that on every piece of paper there's somebody's story, and we've got to deal with that for its human content and not just for its administrative problems. But it is difficult and it's a real struggle to think that my job is not to get all these problems solved, but to accompany people in the problems of living and of trying to live faith, which is different.

I've struggled hard with things like educational matters and the way we understand the meaning of spiritual development right through school. I struggle with people, often in the state sector, who want to identify the spiritual with the religious, and I say, 'Now that won't do. All right, I'm a religious figure, but every person is a spiritual being, and I want to push you to try and think about the spiritual outside the terms of the religious.' So I've written about that, I've talked about that, I've been invited to local authority meetings with five or six hundred teachers to try and explore those kinds of issues and I've had different reactions. I remember one chap came up at the end of a talk and said, 'You are a most dangerous man. I'm a humanist and I will oppose you to my dying day, because I think you're misleading these people. What you're trying to do is lead them on from a spiritual awareness to belief in God.' I said, 'Of course I am. That's what I'm here for, and that's what I believe.' And he retorted, 'Well I don't.'

I said earlier that my father did not intervene or seek to influence me in any way, but I do remember one bit of advice he gave me after ordination. He said, 'My advice to you is this: in the Church, ask for nothing and refuse nothing.' I've quite often thought about that and I think he's right. Speculation about who will be Bishop of here, there or anywhere is largely futile. Normally such speculation is cast, especially by the media, in the mould of speculation about political leadership, in other words in terms of personality, policy stance, support – all that kind of thing. One of the advantages of the Church is that the process by which a bishop is appointed is cooler than that. It's a more distant decision which is totally separate from that kind of speculation and hype. So even though there has been plenty of speculation, I tend to distance myself from it all. I try very hard to close myself off to it and not let it get to me, but sometimes it's a struggle.

I know there's no thrill attached to the job of Archbishop of Westminster. It is a very, very hard task. Watching this Cardinal – the only one I know – I think it takes remarkable qualities to do what he has done, which is to sustain the effort that it requires, *and* retain his humanity and his spirit in the way that he does. There are real lessons to be learnt from Cardinal Hume. Realism about what can be done and what can't be done, and ... oh ... humility's the wrong word. It's not humility. It's that he constantly stands before God rather than before the public. He is not measuring himself by what people think. He really *does* believe that the important measure is as he stands before God, and that, for him, is not a particularly comfortable place. He's not a man who moves easily into spiritual consolation, but he just knows that that's the important task and so he gives himself first to that task of standing before God, and everything else is second to that. I think that's why he's still sane – that's why he's still human. That's why he's still got a real spark about him. Nobody – nobody in their right mind would grasp and seek the office of Cardinal and I certainly don't. I certainly don't.

The issue of child abuse in the Church is awful – there's no doubt at all. The trauma that youngsters go through and carry for the rest of their lives is terrible. It's the kind of activity which is *so* difficult to understand, yet we are only gradually discovering how horrifyingly widespread it is. After all 85 per cent of child abuse takes place within families; it doesn't involve clergy. So the bulk of the problem is not something that involves a priest or a church worker, but that area is also real. We've tried, as the Bishops' Conference in England and Wales, to address how we respond to an accusation of abuse and we were the first ecclesiastical authority to do that. Maybe it seemed as though we took a long time, but we weren't lacking, we weren't neglectful. Then there's the question of how we respond to victims and again there was a separate attempt to address that. At the moment we're working on how we handle people who have abused children. They don't just disappear, they remain and there are very complex issues in that. But there's no doubt it's an area that has burst into the public arena from underground and it's difficult to keep up with the demands of it.

I doubt if there's any institution in this country that has served children as dedicatedly, and I think on balance as well, as the Catholic Church – think of all the adoption agencies and the childcare agencies that have dealt with hundreds of thousands of children when nobody else wanted to know them, quite apart from all the schools. So the balance is still very much that here is a Church that is committed to life and to *vulnerable* life. OK, we've had appalling errors, but I don't think we respond badly to children. There is also the other experience of false accusations and there are enough false accusations made to put one a little bit on one's guard, while quite admitting that the whole balance of probability is that the child who should be believed will not be believed. It's a very serious problem, but we're addressing it continually as best we can.

As bishops, we try to hold the balance between strong opposing views within the Catholic community and that is actually quite a difficult position to take up; it's never the easy one. The easy one is to take up a single strong view and not worry if people don't agree with you. So there is a kind of leadership that is exercised in the Church's public life which requires strength. There are very profound moves and shifts and differences within the Church, and as bishops we should respond to them. But I'm not sure that we would all agree on how to respond. I remember one series of discussions we had about whether it would be a good idea to have many more eucharistic prayers so that when Mass was celebrated there would be a whole range of prayers to choose from. Some say, 'Yes, that's wonderful, because that reflects the diversity and the many-faceted mystery of God.' Others say, 'No, actually what we need in public prayer is something that's very familiar, something that everybody gets to know, something that they can pray their way into through familiarity.' Now personally, the second view would be mine, but we are not of one mind as a body of bishops.

There is an increasing desire for simplicity, a desire for more silence, a desire for more focus on the central mystery of what we're doing, rather than the surrounding accompaniments. I say to parishes, 'Please try and become schools of prayer', and in many of them there is a growing practice of prayer of different sorts. Quite a number of parishes have weeks of guided prayer and retreats woven into everyday life. Many of them have reinstated periods of prayer and adoration of the Blessed Sacrament. These are the beginnings of points of stability that are, as it were, profound enough to bear the mystery of God's presence among us. There's less focus now on how we as a people externally celebrate our faith and a growing understanding that participation does not necessarily mean external activity, like standing up or sitting down, singing, composing prayers or moving about the church. Rather, there is an important participation that is largely interior, or of the heart. This, too, needs to be fostered every time we celebrate the Mass.

The priest is one aspect of the life of the Church which is given. It's there, it's not chosen. Parishes don't choose their priests, they're given a priest. In a sense the priest stands as a symbol that faith is a gift of God, and it is God who is seeking us, and it is God who reveals the life of God to us. We don't discover those things. We do, pedagogically, in our own personal journey, but the initiative is with God. The priest is also an instrument. When I celebrate Mass, I'm very conscious of what is happening; as the prayers suggest, we are asking that through the power of the Holy Spirit these gifts of bread and wine become the body and blood of the Lord. I'm just the instrument of that transaction. God uses me to do something like one might use a biro.

I remember something my father said which has made a deep impression on me. The first Mass I celebrated back in Crosby after my years in Rome was on the Feast of St Peter and St Paul on 29 June – it was a Thursday. Then the following Saturday I went along to talk to the canon who was the parish priest about which Mass I could say on Sunday. I came back home and my father was reading the paper. 'Hey, Dad,' I said, 'I've been down to see the canon and he's asked me to say the ten o'clock Mass tomorrow.'

No reaction. So I went on, 'You know, I'm just saying, I've been to see the canon and he wants me to say the—'

'Yes,' he said, 'I heard, I heard.'

'Well,' I replied, 'I thought you might be interested.'

So he put down his newspaper and he said, 'You'd better understand, I wouldn't go across the road to Mass because you're saying it. I'll go to Mass because it's the Mass, and who the priest is doesn't matter. And anyway,' he says, 'you know I go to the half past five Mass.' Obviously he was making a point. In fact he came to the ten o'clock Mass, but he was saying to me, 'Don't let this thing take hold of you. You're the servant and don't get yourself out of proportion in all of this.' I think that this perspective is coming right back round again in the reflections on priesthood that we've been doing here.

The rewards of priesthood for me are unquestionably in the response of people to this ministry. Without any doubt, it is quite, quite remarkable how much people love their priest, how much they're prepared to tolerate from their priest, and how much support they will give a priest – simply because he's a priest.

11. Father Philip Inch

Fr Philip Inch was born in Liverpool in 1958

Fr Philip Inch, 41, speaks with a soft Liverpudlian accent. His face is regular, his complexion honey-coloured. Clad in civvies and sandals, he reminds me of a gardener – gentle and willowy. But there is also a determination about Fr Philip – perhaps even a wilfulness. As a child, he was loved tenderly by both his parents but his father – a sea captain – was often away. This gave him plenty of unrivalled access to his mother, an arrangement which was interrupted when he was 13 by the return, for good, of his father. Soon after this, the young Philip left for seminary, and the timing, he admits, was more than accidental.

The presbytery Fr Philip lives in is large and he has the house to himself, although he owns virtually nothing in it. The parish is new – he's yet to settle in. It's a typical situation and one that is classically conducive to loneliness; as such he talks about celibacy with unprompted openness. Celibacy, says Fr Philip, is something for the whole community to take on, not just the priest. As a human being, he wants to love and be loved in return. He wants intimacy with men and women. Only then, says Fr Philip, can celibacy be meaningful. This is a risky approach. Most clergy turn to their fellow priests for support and consolation. Having opted for, as it were, 'semi-relationships', Fr Philip describes in this chapter what happens when these relationships work – and when they don't.

My worst moment as a priest was when a woman came to me and said, 'Every time I make love to my husband I think of you, because you've been so kind to me and so caring, and so I think about you when I'm making love to my husband.'

It was completely out of the blue. She said I listened to her in a way that her husband didn't, that I bought her flowers when her husband didn't. I had done. I mean, I can't deny that. I'd obviously listened to her at some stage and she'd been very low, so I'd just bought her a bunch of flowers. And OK, I suppose I would think twice about it now, but I didn't think twice about it then and didn't realize the messages I was giving her. Anyway, I wanted to run a mile. It was just before Easter; I remember it vividly.

I'm a bit of a control freak, so you can imagine the kind of panic I felt in terms of this relationship running completely out of my control. The funny thing about it was that I'd never been particularly close to this woman, I'd never felt I'd got that close to her. She sorted out her relationship with her husband and they're very happily married now, so it resolved itself, but it was a very big lesson to me. I remember wondering what would have happened if I'd felt anything like that about her. If I ever got into that situation again, what would be the outcome?

The very first time I ever told anybody I wanted to be a priest was when I was seven. Her name was Joanna and she was also seven years old and we were sitting on the stairs in her house. My mum was talking to her mum and Joanna said to me, 'Will you marry me?' – like you do at that age. And I said to her, 'No, I can't because I'm going to be a priest,' and she went and told my mum. And that was the very first time I'd ever said to anybody that I wanted to be a priest.

I really did feel I wanted to be a priest. I wasn't just saying it ... in fact, Joanna cried when I said that; it's the only time a girl's ever cried over me. We had a very good priest in our home parish, a man called Kevin Finn who was a big influence on me. He had time to give to people in a way that I feel I've never had as a priest. We had a choir and altar service and he used to take us away on holidays – all over the place. And I used to think, 'Yes, I want to be like that.'

When I was 11 I wanted to go to the junior seminary because somehow I'd heard that if you wanted to be a priest, that's where you had to go. I remember saying to my mum, 'I want to go,' and she said to me, 'If you wanted to be a train driver, I wouldn't send you to live in Liverpool's Lime Street Station at the age of 11; I'd tell you to wait. So I'm going to tell you the same.' Obviously I must have pestered her because in the end, when I was 13, I went to the junior seminary at Upholland, which was a boarding school.

It was horrible. My first impressions were horrific because we had nothing of our own. All we had was a bed and one drawer. There wasn't even a chair to sit on. I remember lying in bed on the first night. My dad had taken me there in the car and the image I retained was of my mum standing on the front doorstep at home and crying as I left. I remember lying in bed that first night and thinking, 'This is the most stupid thing I've ever done. I've left home, a nice comfortable home, and I've left everything I know, and I've come here.' I'm not – it probably sounds daft – I'm not into visions, but ... that night I know that Our Lady said to me, 'Well, don't worry, I'm your mum as well and I'll look after you.'

Sometimes you just know something. I didn't hear a voice. I didn't have an apparition. But I just knew, somehow, that I would be all right. It was a conviction. Five days later my mum went into hospital to have a baby, and a woman came into the hospital ward. My mum didn't know her and still doesn't know her to this day, but she said to my mum, 'God's taken one from you and he's given you back another one in his place.' To this day we don't know who she was.

I remember a time at the seminary when I had to make a decision about whether or not I would stay. There was a girl who I had become very fond of, I mean, more than very fond of really. We had long holidays and we'd become very close. It was Joanna in fact – Joanna again. I knew I had to make a decision. I knew I couldn't dangle her along any more; it was one of those decisive moments. At that time Archbishop Worlock used to have a reunion for seminarians every Christmas and we had to go to it. We all hated it because we were on holiday but we had to go. This one particular year there was a woman – Margaret – who'd been invited to give us some talks. She was very charismatic, not in terms of her personality but in her religion. She was a married woman from Ireland and was very into charismatic renewal.

She spoke and spoke very well but the minute she'd finished, everybody left the room as quickly as they could – everybody,

I mean everybody. So I was left in the room with her on my own and I just wanted to be with everybody else. But I thought, 'Well, we can't just leave her, you know, on her own.' So I sat with her while everybody else went to the pub. I sat with this woman and I talked to her. And for some reason I started talking to her about this decision I had to make. I don't really talk to strangers about personal things – unless they ask me to. I mean, I don't. But I talked to her and I said to her, 'I've got to make this decision. It feels like God wants all of me. It feels like I'm going to a bank and handing everything in, and I'm really not sure what I'm going to get back.' Now she didn't know me at all but I can remember her words to me. She said, 'Well, I've one thing to say to you and it's this. I know that God wants every inch of you to be a priest.' She could not have known my name was Philip *Inch*. It was one of those little moments when God reveals God's self to you, and what God wants.

I think if I'd married Joanna it would have opened up lots of possibilities, both for her and for me; lots of doors would have opened. And yet, if the Church said tomorrow that celibacy could be optional, I would still choose the option to remain celibate because I think it allows me to be available to other people in different kinds of ways.

If I was married and had a wife and children, I would have to give time and energy to them, and that would mean giving less time and energy to the work and the parish or whatever it is I'm doing. So it's the availability of energy. And I think the pressures on a married priest – the burdens of guilt about where to spend quality time – would be immense. I'm sure it's the same for anybody in any kind of work situation, so it's not peculiar to priesthood. But the fact that I am not married means that I am freer to give time and energy to other things which I would otherwise want to give to a wife and family.

What it means to be a priest certainly came home to me very clearly in a television programme called *Boys from the Blackstuff*. There was a very powerful scene in there about the death of a character called George Malone. The priest is there, you know, doing all the Catholic ritual, and in the middle of his sermon Chrissie, the son, stands up and says, 'Look father, cut the crap. We're not here to hear all this. I know it's your job, but we're here to celebrate the life of my father.' That was first on television, I think, in 1980, and was repeated again in the year I was ordained. And I thought that summed up exactly what being a priest is about for me. It's not about piously bringing God into people's lives. It's about helping people to recognize the presence of God *already in* their lives, and bringing people to celebrate that presence. Very clearly, that's what it's about. So I'm helping people to realize the presence of God. I'm actually saying, 'Let's celebrate that, and strengthen it and renew it and deepen it.'

You can bring people to celebrate the presence of God in all sorts of different ways, and not just through church. That's why there's always a big debate about funerals and whether or not people should be allowed to have pop music at them. They want a song. Should I allow it? Well, I'm very reluctant to say no because for those people that song has a deep meaning. I've got to help them see that God is still part of their celebration. I'm not bringing God into it, I'm pointing out the presence of God; it's what I call 'kingdom-spotting'.

The greatest challenge to me as a priest is how I live – authentically – a gospel way of life. That affects everything that I do: my lifestyle, my personal needs, my relationships. It's about the way I preach and the way I live as a priest in the world, and I don't feel I've ever really grasped the challenge of that properly.

At one stage I lived in a parish where my work was in St Mary's, Highfield Street in the centre of Liverpool. I was working mainly for the business community since it had the remnants of the days when Highfield Street attracted a lot of business people to a weekday Mass. There was also a very small resident population. It was a very depopulated area and very poor, and people lived in the most horrendous housing you could imagine. There were a lot of derelict flats. People used to wake up in the morning and find their water tanks had been stolen for the lead so there'd be water everywhere. They kept their houses and their flats beautifully, but the walkways and the stairwells up to them were horrendous. There were always broken windows, broken bottles, vandalism ... And yet, out of that came really good people. I don't know how people lived like that, in such terrible situations.

I thought, 'How can I identify with the lives of these people who I'm living with?' I decided that I would live on the collection that came in on a Sunday and that was about ... well, it was between £23 and £35 a week. I was still getting the salary, but I decided that for the actual living expenses I would only live on whatever came in.

As a priest I get a minimum diocesan salary. I can't remember what it was then but it's now £3,300 a year. But our actual living expenses are paid for by the parish, so that's separate to the salary which pays for things like a car, holidays and clothes. The parish pays for things like the phone bill, the heating, the lighting and food. Living on the collection was quite difficult. In fact it was very difficult. It meant I couldn't eat meat. And there were times when I literally didn't have enough money to go out and buy some milk. I had to be very careful about how many phone calls I made. It was a decision I made in order to try to say to the people who lived in that area, 'I want to live in the same way that everybody else lives here. I want to share the difficult life you're living.' I did that for 18 months. Nobody would ever have known. It was just something I felt I should do.

Being a priest is a very privileged existence. I don't have any worries about mortgages or redundancy. I don't have all the stresses and strains of parenthood and bringing up children. So how do I live a vocation to love as a celibate priest? That's the challenge. I think I try to do it like a candle. Maybe it's not a good image but a candle gives light and warmth, but it also costs the candle something; the candle gets smaller and smaller. I try to live the vocation to love by giving as much of me as possible to wherever I am. There are times when I think, 'Well, why should I do this? People don't actually care for me as a person, so why should I spend my time caring for them?' Celibacy is not just something that the priest takes on alone, it's something that the whole community takes on as well. I think people have a responsibility to love a priest. If we are going to have a celibate priesthood, the community and the parish have a responsibility towards their priest. It's not just about supporting him, it's about love.

We walk a difficult tightrope. We've all been in situations where the boundaries have been crossed in ways that perhaps they shouldn't have been, and that's the risk we take. But I don't see any other way of living the priesthood. I mean, I've tried. I've

FAITH, HOPE AND CHASTITY

tried to live it other ways. Other priests do and I'm not criticizing them. Some clergy find all their strength and support from other priests and they're very complete in that. But for me, if I make a commitment to be in a parish, to be with people, then I'm saying, 'I'm here, all of me is here, and that has implications for you as well as for me.'

I need to feel as though I've got a part to play in people's lives. I need to feel as though I matter to people, that people actually care for me as Philip Inch. I need to be loved by people, to be intimate with people, because celibacy doesn't deny intimacy. And I need to be intimate with women as well as men. I've experienced the joy of this kind of love but also the pain of it. It can go wrong.

The time did come when, as a priest, I fell in love with a woman. At first I used to pray that the husband would die ... that seemed like the easiest option. I had to work through things. I mean, if you're honest with yourself in terms of the way you feel – and you don't always have to be honest with the other person – then I think you can work through those kinds of situation. I said to myself, 'Yes, I have fallen in love and I have allowed that to happen. And now I've got to fall out of love.' 'Fall out of love' is probably the wrong expression, but I think one can decide to love somebody in a different way. I was fortunate that the situation was such that my love for that woman became a love that embraced her and all her family. I would say that I still love her, but I also love her husband and children, we are good friends. But it may not have ended that way.

As a priest you're invited into people's lives to share moments and times with them that nobody else is privileged to in the same kind of way. And they're not just moments of birth and death and marriage but moments when people really invite you to be part of their families, their celebrations, their difficult times. That's a very deep privilege, to be part of that. I used to think that the longer I was a priest the easier it would get, in terms of being certain about it, but actually the reverse is true. The longer I'm a priest, the more I question whether I should remain a priest. I suppose there are moments in my life when I think, 'Well, I'm 41 ... if I want to leave and stop doing this, I'd better do it soon, because otherwise I'll be too old.' I love children – that is a big sacrifice; I would love to have children. Maybe it's because I'm reaching those kinds of milestones that it gets more difficult. It doesn't seem to get easier to remain committed to priesthood.

But having said all that, I'm still here, I am committed to it and I think, 'Well, if I wasn't a priest, what would I miss?' The thing I would miss most would be celebrating Mass, not on my own – because I think if I wasn't a priest I'd still sneak in and do it on my own somewhere – but being with a congregation, and leading them in the celebration of Mass. Maybe I should say Mass and the sacraments, because I think it's such a holy moment when God and human beings are brought into an intimate relationship; to lead that in a sensitive way for me is so important. It's also exhausting. I always say to people, 'Unless you're a priest, you could never realize how exhausting it is to celebrate Mass, because in some way you take upon yourself the prayers of the people who are there; you lead them in their prayerful relationship with God.' But it's also a deeply spiritual and privileged experience.

In celebrating Mass I feel the responsibility – personally – of a task of prayer, not just for me but for others. That's clearly shown in the celebration of Mass, not only in the words we use but in the fact that in some way I am re-enacting what Our Lord himself did on the Cross, when his ultimate act of love for others was his death. So in my own little way, I'm becoming part of that in celebrating Mass. It's something much bigger than me – it's the choirs of heaven and all the angelic hosts – it's the holy bit in terms of the Book of Revelation. I'm caught up in something that makes me feel very small, very insignificant, and yet also makes me feel immensely privileged and *powerful* as well. I hesitate to use the word, but it does. We're keying into something that's so much bigger than just that particular moment in time. It's something so much bigger than all that. It's a moment of communion, not just with God, not just with people, but with everything that's gone before us, and in a funny kind of way with everything that's yet to come. There's a real sense of ministry and service in the celebration of the Mass – things of earth touch things of heaven. It's what a priest is for.

12. Stuart Carney

Stuart Carney was born in Durham in 1973

Stuart Carney is training to be a Jesuit. I met him right at the start of his novitiate, a process which can take 20 years or longer before producing the fruit of a fully fledged Jesuit. His interview reflects this. At once sad and optimistic, Stuart Carney mourns both the past he has left behind and the future he has sacrificed.

I first heard about this trainee priest through a mutual friend who raved about Stuart as being one of the most outstandingly brilliant boys at the monastic boarding school which they both attended. Stuart was indeed an exceptional scholar, achieving 11 GCSEs, two AO levels, four A levels and one AS level – all with top grades. Destined for a glittering career in medicine and having qualified at Edinburgh University, Stuart chose the Church instead – to the amazement of his friends and the dismay of his mother.

Physically and verbally Stuart is the epitome of a well educated and confident public school boy. Occasionally referring to himself in the third person, he falls just short of arrogance, and although I warmed to him immediately, others may take longer to sympathize. I liked him because although his intellect is formidable it in no way masks his vulnerability. Stuart's stories of 'fagging' at school, together with his determination later on to remain celibate, reveal a soul clearly tortured by the demands of his faith in a secular and often amoral world.

Tall, dark and intense, Stuart Carney will arouse passion wherever he goes. I once asked him whether he ever felt depressed. 'Depressed?' he said. 'Never. Despair, often.'

The aspect of school which I found particularly despicable was the culture of 'fagging'. It was a system of abuse, of bullying, of sixth formers using first formers to tidy their rooms, bring them breakfast, empty their bins, go to the tuckshop, run errands, do this, do that, make coffees – until eleven, twelve, one o'clock in the morning – for them and all of their friends who'd congregate in the house. At the age of 13 or 14 I'd be woken up, or kept up, to do all of this. In addition I'd be required to wake these people in the morning and invariably someone would throw an ashtray which would narrowly miss me. I think the novel or film which best portrays it is *The Lord of the Flies*. There was very much an attitude of 'it happened to me, therefore it should happen to you', and this was expressed by my housemaster when my parents first arrived. 'Your son,' he said, 'will be expected to do this for senior boys, and when he is in the sixth form he will be able to get the junior boys to do this for him.' It was legitimate and approved of – it was part of the system. But Stuart was stubborn and Stuart was homesick. He hadn't really entered into the way of the house, and further to that he avoided as much of this as he could.

Bullying took many forms – being pinned to beds was one of them. I'd be lying in bed at night and people would either jump on me from the top of wardrobes or my bed would be 'lamp-posted', in other words turned up on its side with me in it. Saturdays were particularly unpleasant in the house because of the drinking. The idea was that people could go off to the pub to have a meal and a couple of pints. A couple of pints, however, became three, four, five, six, seven ... so on a Saturday evening the house would be carnage and I knew I would be summoned down to the TV room to do something for one of the senior boys. There was one particular incident when I was held up against a wall while older boys threw snooker balls at me; these left imprints on the walls either side of my head. You can still see them in the wall, almost like a small silhouette where a first-year boy – me – had been standing. I don't think the homesickness ever fully left me; I just began to accept it, to tolerate it and I suppose to become a little immune to it. I learnt strategies for coping.

My mother saw how unhappy I was at school and now has deep regrets about it; she fears that her impressionable son may in some way have been unduly influenced by all of this. But like all parents – and she says this with the greatest sincerity, love and devotion – all she wants is her son's and her daughter's happiness. As Dad said to me recently, 'If you do get ordained, you should know that the proudest person sitting in the congregation will be your mother.' But she was initially angry about my decision to become a Jesuit and denied it for a long time. 'Surely,' she used to say, 'you could be of equal service as a doctor, and a married man with children.' She finds the whole thing very tough, but I know of the love that she has for me.

I think the possibility of a vocation had always been a joke when I was at school. A lot of people would throw around the idea of 'Stuart Carney OSB'. Indeed, certain members of the monastic community approached me and said to me, 'Have you ever thought of joining us?' The idea didn't really appeal to me because of the emotional baggage that I was carrying. This was a place where I had been desperately unhappy, therefore any psychiatrist would be asking why I was going to prolong the agony.

My father flirted with the idea of joining the Jesuits himself. I remember being very touched by one of the comments he made when we were discussing all of this. 'Now Stuart,' he said, 'I think you'll probably make a good doctor. But if the priesthood is what you feel called to do then so be it. Perhaps my vocation is your vocation. Perhaps it was *my* vocation to meet your mother, fall in love with your mother, marry her and have you.' That whole idea really touched me. I think my father feels in a slightly difficult position. He doesn't want to show too much emotion for fear of upsetting my mother, who is not a Catholic. Her greatest dread when I went to a monastic boarding school was that I would want to become a priest. She worried about the adage attributed to the Jesuits, 'Give me a child until the age of seven and I'll have him for the rest of his life.' She felt that her son would be in some way brainwashed or manipulated into doing something against his will. So Mum finds the whole thing very strange and looks at it very much as an outsider.

I found the institutional life of school quite strange. The dormitories in the house were primitive – it was like sleeping in horseboxes. The furniture was pretty spartan and had been vandalized by previous generations of boys. I was one of the few scholars in the house, which was a very rugby-focused one, and I think I retreated into my shell. I felt pretty left out of it. I was in a year which had been fed from the junior house so slightly more than half of the other boys already knew each other. The fact that I got a scholarship meant that I felt under a certain amount of pressure to keep up the work, and that went quite against the grain of my house. The very fact that Stuart should be sitting at his 'carrel' – or desk – and working was perceived in some way as a threat. Here was this boy, swimming against the flow. But I could have brought a bit of it upon myself as well by virtue of my stubbornness. I wasn't prepared to give in or to play the boyish pranks and get drunk at weekends and all of that. I was seen as standing a bit aloof. I was suffering.

I had been thinking about medicine since I was 13. I loved the sciences and had a sense that I wanted to do something of service which involved working directly with people. I didn't want to go into a laboratory-based discipline, so medicine fitted the bill. Also, whenever I suggested being a solicitor like my father, my mother would say, 'Well, what about medicine?' To my mother, medicine is the most noble of the professions. When I was 16 I first felt I may have a vocation to the priesthood, however because I didn't have the courage or the certainty to deal with it, medicine became the focus. Certainly I was thinking about a vocation and praying about it but my father and friends at school quite rightly said, 'Go to medical school first. If it's a true vocation from God, it will withstand medical school. Furthermore, if you are to become a religious or a priest, you'll give greater service if you have professional qualifications as well. If it's *not* what God is calling you to, you will still be of great service as a doctor.'

My interest in the Jesuits was initially partly to do with the fact that I enjoyed the reaction I provoked on mentioning them to the monks at school. It was a bit like mentioning *Macbeth* in the theatre. They would engage in a kind of ritual and say, 'Oh no, you can't possibly do that. Haven't you heard about their past and all the things the Jesuits get up to?' One particular individual who was trying to turn me off the Society said, 'One of the things the Jesuits do is a "manifestation of conscience" annually to the Provincial. What happens if you don't like your Provincial?

Would you really want to tell him what's been bothering you?' Everybody seemed to have an opinion of the Society; there was clearly an aspect of the Jesuit life which was not consistent with Benedictine spirituality. So that inflamed my curiosity and could have been, in this one aspect, my own little rebellion.

My final A level year was particularly stressful because I was head of house. I'd managed to get a conditional place at Cambridge to read Medicine but I didn't get the grades. I think that was probably the first time I had failed in something. I felt cheated, having slogged away for so many years, but I went to Edinburgh and in fact it was fabulous. I was wide-eyed. Having emerged from an all-male Catholic boarding school, I arrived in heaven; it was a brilliant time. I had a wide circle of friends who were superb people and great drinking buddies, and I thoroughly enjoyed my time up in Edinburgh – socially it was out of this world. I felt liberated, as though a huge burden had been taken away. I remembered how at school I would start the term well-fed and well-nourished but by the end of the term I'd have lost, say, a stone, maybe a stone and a half because I was so stressed. None of these troubles upset my time in Edinburgh. It was a tremendous experience and I wouldn't change it for the world. Once I had acquired a professional qualification I felt in a far stronger position. To a certain extent I had proved to myself that I could make it and so could go on to do what I really wanted to do.

Medicine is such a privileged profession. The friendships that developed as a consequence of that experience were profound and the insights I got into personal suffering were incredible. I remember one lady who had motor neurone disease and was unable to speak. I decided that she should be one of my long-term cases for an assessment in neurology and I struggled for a couple of hours to get a history out of her by writing messages on paper. She was a tremendous woman of great courage and dignity, with a beautiful face and a fabulous smile. I am not sure why she made such an impression on me, except that in spite of all her suffering she never lost her sense of humour. She died shortly after my attachment to the ward. And then there was a lady in my surgical attachment as a house officer, who I visited on my day off after playing a round of golf because the day before she'd been quite upset. We discussed her worries about whether her cancer had come back or whether the previous operation had been a success. She was understandably very upset about all of this. But there was nothing I could say because I couldn't answer any of her questions; they could only be answered by further exploratory procedures. When she was about to be discharged, she called me over at the end of a ward round and stuffed a set of golf balls and tees into the pocket of my white coat. That really stuck with me; it was one those 'YES!' experiences. I felt affirmed and thanked for doing something I thoroughly enjoyed. That was quite incredible and I couldn't possibly exchange it for anything.

The more fun I had at Edinburgh in the first couple of years, the less I thought about vocation. After two years, however, the vocation hadn't gone away so I summoned sufficient courage one day after Mass to go and speak to a Jesuit priest – Frank Barnet – who organized a spiritual director for me. My first director, Lawrence Nam, was a great man but I really didn't get the hang of Ignatian spirituality. The way I worked at medical school was to have a superb three or four weeks and then a three-day blitz on work as I crammed for the next exam. In the same way, instead of really giving over a period of time each day to prayer, I would look at the suggested biblical passages in the hour before going off for spiritual direction, and then try and work out the thread to them all. I'd come up with what I thought was a very intellectual exegesis as to what the passages could be saying but my ideas were rapidly rejected. 'Have you actually prayed in the last month, Stuart?' Lawrence would say. He was very good for me and very patient.

My experience up to this point had included a few episodes of really feeling that God was talking to me, of being loved by God and of feeling that I could love others as a consequence of this. I remember one occasion, walking back through the lofty corridors of the Royal Infirmary in Edinburgh just after a patient had died at two in the morning. I felt pretty down but I had a great sense that somebody was walking with me. There was a warmth, not just a gooey feeling but a sense that I was not alone, that somebody was with me – physically.

I had relationships with women in Edinburgh, although not initially of particularly long duration. There were some brilliant women who I would date and go to the cinema with and get intimate with as well. But I'd decided that if I had a true vocation, people could only get so close. I was still struggling with the idea of a vocation and one of my biggest regrets is that I didn't really allow people to get too close. I suppose my relationships with girls, with women, were the same as a teenager's. They were reasonably close and reasonably intimate although I never really fell madly and passionately in love – I never allowed myself to. I agonized over having a sexual relationship – over the propriety of whatever relationship I was engaged in – and made a deliberate decision not to lose my virginity. Thus far and no further. With hindsight I regret that I made such a big issue of it and that I did not enter more fully into the relationships at university.

A life of celibacy is at times a daunting prospect. However, it facilitates everything the Jesuits do: the living in community, the mobile existence and the diversity of the work we're engaged in. I'm beginning to derive great strength and support from the community here, which to a certain extent addresses some of my emotional needs. Some of my other emotional needs are addressed as far as my relationship with God, through prayer, is concerned. But I think celibacy will be tough.

'Appropriate intimacy' is a buzzword which I'm currently trying to come to terms with and I suppose using a buzzword is rather cheating on my part. I remember talking with a friend recently about this and he asked me what I missed about relationships. I miss the chase, and then the moment of realizing that the woman you've been chasing feels the same for you. And then the intimacy beyond that, yes, I miss that. I miss the intimacy of relationships. But nobody seems to be saying, 'Stuart, from now on you must be very careful in your dealings with women and keep them at arm's length.' If they did, I think I would probably pack my bags and suggest I find some other way of working out my vocation. Once again, it's partly a question of discipline but also of trying to work out for myself how far I want to go. I think we must be fair to the people we're talking to; Jesuits don't tend to wear identifying clothes, for instance. But yes, I'm beginning to grapple with temptations. I may fall in love. I will cross that bridge if or when it comes.

At this stage in my formation I have a great sense of being called to serve the Church as a Jesuit. Priesthood is the next stage and that's all part of equipping myself with the tools to be of greater service – a bit like working in the Health Service and then becoming a consultant. As a priest, I will be ordained to perform a particular task – bringing the sacraments to people – but I will also be teaching, visiting the sick and working in schools and prisons, all of which can be done equally well by lay people. But becoming a Jesuit priest is something other, something different, something rather mysterious which I think is all tied up with service.

I think what I hope to bring to others over the next 50 or 60 years is a sense of God's love, for it is my love of God and the experience of God's love for me that drives and energizes me. The model I have for this is the great love my parents have for each other and for my sister and me. Similarly I'm in love with God, and I hope that I'll be able to share that, not necessarily by going on and on about it but by my very demeanour, by the way I live and work with other people. If I achieved nothing else, I would hope to inspire people with a sort of contagious enthusiasm and to share some of that love with others; it's something that I have received and am very grateful for, but it's not just for me. If in some way I can touch somebody else's heart with that love affair with God, then the next 50 or 60 years won't be misplaced.

Since the time of this interview Stuart Carney has left the Jesuit novitiate.

13. Father Arthur Fitzgerald

Fr Arthur Fitzgerald was born in Liverpool in 1946

My meeting with Fr Arthur Fitzgerald sped by in a whirl of words, anecdotes and information. A tall, lean man with a craggy face and furrowed brow, Fr Arthur rattled through his story at top speed, leaving me to unravel its many folds in my own good time. Later on, as I read through the text, I found myself surprisingly moved by his words. For Fr Arthur – otherwise known as 'Fitz' – idealism is the oxygen, the motor house, which drives his priesthood. As the very stuff of which he is made, it is both inspiring and disturbing.

Fr Arthur has actively supported four British women, including Andrea Needham and Jo Wilson, who broke into a BAe armaments factory and proceeded to inflict thousands of pounds' worth of damage on Hawk jets. As part of the 'Ploughshares' movement[1] which takes its cue from the Bible, they set out to literally beat the weapons into symbolic ploughshares. Fr Arthur himself has broken into an armaments factory, an action for which he was arrested and later faced trial.

What motivates this priest to break the law and is he right to do so? These are two of the many questions answered in this chapter – a chapter which tells the story of a man who describes himself as a coward and yet whose very fear and timidity of life have motivated him to challenge it at every turn.

---

[1] 'Ploughshares' is an international movement of non-violent direct action, taking its mandate from Micah 4:1–4 and Isaiah 2:4 to hammer weapons into 'ploughshares', or tools for nourishment.

The prophetic action by four British women of disarming a Hawk jet was incredible. An action like that is truly prophetic when someone gives themselves totally to it – it's something to do with life and death – there's an almost foolish self-giving in the process; that's a prophetic action. Jesus did it. These British women did it. The prophets did it. These kinds of action call everyone who hears about them to decide and act. We decided. We acted.

I don't see this kind of action as breaking the law, I see it as an experience of conversion – a real Gospel experience – of being exposed and evangelized by the poor. Being evangelized by the poor doesn't just mean putting money in a box so that some cattle project gets an extra £10 or something. Being evangelized by the poor means setting up the kind of accommodation and welcome that actually says, 'The world has to be converted.' Not 'I'm all right, everyone else has to be converted.' It means knowing that power and resources can only be redeemed when the perspective and agenda of the poor is welcomed. If this leads to conviction and action, then conversion is happening. All of us have to be converted by meeting each other's needs. In that process we are disturbed and in that disturbance we meet conversion. We live it. I certainly lived it through that Easter, and I took it over the fence with me when I broke into the armaments factory. I don't see that as lawbreaking. I think law is very, very important. It's the backbone of society; without it we collapse. I'm not generally a lawbreaker but I am driven by the Gospel. And if the Gospel is suppressed by the way the law is at the moment, then it's the law that needs to be challenged.

I was brought up in a family where my father, an Irishman, had very strict and simple views of family roles. Mum was the mother and housewife and he was the breadwinner and ruler. After my mother died the eldest girls had to play their role with my eldest brother, who worked in the same factory as my father, eventually taking the opposite shift in order to be able to keep a male at home. Courageously, but not necessarily kindly, my father put together decades of caring for his family – alone but not without conflict.

My first conscious memory is probably of being sat on my mother's lap as she read what I thought were scary stories – fairy tales in other words. I know the importance of people being able to work through what's scary and uncertain to them in a secure atmosphere and I think on my mum's lap that was worked out. As a child I was shy and retiring – I can't think of a reason why, it's just the way I was. I was the first of six children so I should have been robust enough. I thought the priesthood might be a convenient way of entering into adult life, a very safe and comfortable way of living that wouldn't make demands on me.

Mum and Dad were devastated. Mum knew she was going to have to let go of me at a premature time. I was the firstborn and dearly loved; it set me up for life, that love of me. I've always had underlying self-assurance because of that and I know she just hated the idea of me going away. I persisted even though other people tried to put me off. I don't know where that strength came from. I had the quite selfish notion at the age of about nine or ten that I could overcome four or five major adults in my life and still achieve what they thought wasn't wise.

I was brought up in a very secure family but Dad was disappointed that his first child wasn't a girl, and I think that continued. I never quite came up to his expectations. Thank God he's been the one who survived. He's elderly now and I'm the only one here in Liverpool – all the others have left. It means I'm left with the opportunity to work out what needs to be worked out between us and I think we've probably come to terms with most of it. I managed to work things out with Mum while she was still alive. My teenage memories are of sharing the ironing together, making a cup of tea, sitting together and talking during vacations. I know that I'm wanted and loveable because of that experience.

I'd say I look back on two things: the reassurance of Mum's love – total and unconditional – and the uneasiness of not yet having pleased my Dad. Not an unhappy combination of influences in my childhood, both of which left me with a sort of motivation. One of my other siblings is the same – Geraldine, the fifth child. So the first and the fifth children talk to each other and we say how we're still trying to win Dad's approval, which I think in latter years – he's 82 now – he concedes.

I can remember the early days at Upholland seminary. For that timid child it all felt cold and distant, travelling through a seminary with large architecture and miles and miles of corridors – single file here, there and everywhere. And then getting letters from Mum every week, and not opening them immediately until I'd gone into the WC and closed the door and could weep over them. Being away from home as a teenager in a single-sex atmosphere was very strange and I'm sure it postponed whole elements of my development.

I've never regretted being a priest but I think training for the priesthood could have been different. I sometimes feel that being in an all-male environment, celibate even before puberty, has meant that my development ended up the wrong way round on occasions. But I don't ever regret being a priest. I think it's the most marvellous thing to have practised a prayer-life, naturally, from the age of 12, and to have time and space for it in the routine. I didn't always appreciate it at the time of course, but I'm deeply grateful for that pattern, that imprint. It was in the fifth and sixth form that I first glimpsed the excitement of Scripture and began to see personally God's relationship with all of us. I thought to myself, 'God, even if I'm only mediocre and clumsy, I want to share this with other people. This is the way of life I want to live.'

I was ordained in 1972 as the document *Justice in the World* came out: the briefest document ever to come out of Rome, it became my manifesto. The whole Church was going through a watershed. We lived in a bit of a bubble in which the strictness and severity of previous roles were in flux, but people hadn't yet reclaimed what they were going to teach and how they were going to form people. There was a middle period when no one was certain of anything but there was a lot of enthusiasm for the Vatican Council, for this new kind of *aggiornamento*, or renewal. We were trained and ordained and practised our first ministry in that atmosphere, before it all closed down. A bunch of us came through from that time and I know some people call us mavericks, but I feel so privileged to have been part of that moment of recreation and truth, I really do.

In one of my first parishes I did a lot of hospital work, especially in casualty and the intensive care unit. I remember a particular incident in the casualty unit at Whiston Hospital. A guy had had a heart attack, and, as you see on telly nowadays, all these people were milling around, everyone was shouting instructions and there was all this electrical stuff going on –

bodies jumping off the table and the rest of it. I was trying to get through this crowd to put some oil on the man's forehead, feeling very important and at least knowing that this was pretty essential when one of the doctors yelled at me, 'He's exhausted. You, you've only just come in. You get up here and help.' I had to stand on this stool and press this guy's chest and jump on him according to instructions, all the time surrounded by this great frantic activity of trying to keep the person alive. It made me see priesthood in perspective.

In hospital, alongside families who were hurt and staff who were sometimes confused after pain, my role as a priest and a believer was important. I remember one particular occasion when a family had been called into hospital in the early hours of a Sunday morning. They'd lost all four of their children in a fire together with literally everything but the night clothes they had on when they arrived. The dad had gone into the fire twice to try and get the children out of the bedroom, but he hadn't succeeded. The staff at that time, for all their competence, hadn't brought these two parents together and were even pussyfooting around by not telling them that their children had died. I remember being quite angry and feeling it was important that we got these two people in the same room, talking to each other. The staff trusted me enough to bring those parents together after allowing them to know, through their own questions really, that the children hadn't survived. That's done internally now in hospitals, but at that time we were all working it out together.

In that parish in Whiston I made a conscious decision that people weren't to be left naïve when it came to the Scriptures. If you're not careful, sermons and pastoral work can be so soft and sugary that they don't ever call people to the dignity and challenge of the Gospel – how to work and how to live. The formation of my priesthood owes as much to the Cardijn Method of 'See, Judge and Act'[2] as it does to seminary training.

---

[2] Joseph Cardijn, c.1920s, trained young workers in a method of responsible faith that led to pastoral action through analysis. Later called the 'Pastoral Cycle', it influenced the Council of Vatican II, cf. *Apostolicum Actuositatum* § 29; *Octogesima Adveniens.* § 4; *Convenientes ex Universo* § 51, 52.

When the poll tax was inflicted upon people, a most unjust tax if ever there was one, I knew people were hurt so I called them together in the parish to actually reflect on how they felt about it. They turned up and they wanted to do something about it. Driven by Catholic social teaching, I knew we shouldn't do things alone but should work with other agencies; because we're Church people, it's easy to feel pure and good and to think that our ways are the best ways. We got involved in local campaigns and as we met people who were politically militant and aggressively active, we found, quite surprisingly, that we had a different way of doing things. We'd often want to come away and review whether we should persist in an action which sometimes felt too aggressive. Other people found a great power in this Church group that was driven by its faith.

At that time a group of parishioners and myself frequently went to court in order to accompany other people. We set up a helpline for people, went to court on our own behalf, confronted magistrates and read Catholic social teaching as part of our defence in court as to why we wouldn't pay the poll tax. People are usually frightened of social action and faith going together. At the beginning of coming into a parish, I step right back, as it were, in my own personal practice. During my first year here, for example, at St Michael's, I was told that I was too political in what I was saying. I tried to withdraw a bit, but I kept that promise I'd made in Whiston that I wouldn't ever water things down – I would say what I really believed was important. It took three or four years of trying to have more and more courage on my part, and more and more willingness on the people's part to hear the Gospel – to actually hear what it calls us to be, now in our times. I started by calling people to notice third world poverty at home. We responded to poverty here in Liverpool by setting up a local credit union and that really socialized people.

Then in January of '96, together with some local trade union people, we set up a 'telephone tree' in order to show our support for four British women, jailed in Lytham for damaging Hawk jets. A 'telephone tree' is a way of networking whereby one person phones a group of people who then each phone a further group of people which includes the police station. The result is tens, if not hundreds of phone calls to the police station. I'd heard of one of these women, a local person called Jo Wilson.

I supported the 'telephone tree' and eventually went to visit the women in Risley. At this point it was decided that the trial should take place in Liverpool as opposed to Preston, since Warton British Aerospace, or BAe, employs many people from the Preston area and it was felt that a jury could be prejudiced. The amount of support that went on around that trial through four or five parishes was absolutely incredible. I believe our parish was about ready for that. That's when we set up our own Catholic Worker.[3]

Later on, when the local community heard the story of Timor, they decided to act. Timor was annexed by Indonesia over 21 years ago in defiance of any number of United Nations resolutions and yet the rest of the world has turned its back on that situation. This, together with the sale of Hawk jets to Indonesia, was what these four women had come to highlight. The women of our parish, the people who have time to go to daily Mass – the elderly and the retired – heard the story and saw a film by John Pilger the investigative human rights journalist, which included the massacre of young people attending the funeral of one of their friends. This took place just before the installation of our new Archbishop, Patrick Kelly. At this meeting, the women of the parish got up and said, 'Everyone who goes to the installation of Pat Kelly must know about these things.' These elderly and middle-aged ladies leafletted every door of the Cathedral. That was when I knew the community was moving and I could move with them.

For ten days outside the trial there were memorial prayers, photographs, Buddhist drumbeating ... it was all very prayerful, very quiet, very respectful. I said Mass outside the trial on one day and white crosses were taped to a series of metal bollards surrounding the forecourt. The moral questions arising from the case were put forward by faith-based people, not only Catholics but the peace movement as well. I can remember the moment we needed to hold back on the trade unionists because they had a different way of

---

[3] The Catholic Worker Movement was founded by Dorothy Day (1897–1980), a Roman Catholic lay woman who was indomitable in her work for peace and human rights. One of the driving forces behind the movement in this country has been Ciaron O'Reilly, a founder member of Brisbane Catholic Worker, Australia. He took part in a Ploughshares action in 1991 in the United States to disarm a B52 bomber, and has frequently been jailed for resistance.

protesting; it was a particular mood and quality to protesting that we wanted to express. That was very important and was based on the Catholic Worker way of being radically Catholic.

The women were acquitted – an unbelievable moment for the whole world. At that moment, when the women were acquitted, solidarity was felt right across the world. I remember reading out a letter in church from some women in Timor to the women in jail, saying how they couldn't believe that their plight as peasants in the mountains of Timor was being remembered by British people who were risking all but their lives. These four British women were heading for four, five, six years in jail – they were already doing six months in jail. The Timorese women were deeply moved by this and felt so encouraged by it on the other side of the world. There was not a dry eye in our Liverpool church as I read their words. Communion at that Mass was especially tangible.

There was rejoicing in Timor on the day of the acquittal and we were part of it. There's solidarity for you. That is probably one of the most exciting things that has ever happened to me. It affirmed what I've worked for all my life, what I think the Gospel calls us to, namely that if anyone is in need, their need is to be answered. After the acquittal of the women, one of them, Andrea Needham, came to live here at the parish for a while. She helped set up a Catholic Worker community and the parish community responded. In the November of that year, Timorese people also came to live with us – two young men who were exiled and for whom it was too dangerous to go back. Portugal had given them European status and now they were looking for places to live in Europe in order to keep the issues of Timor alive.

These two young men have given us the experience of being evangelized by the poor. Solidarity has taken off – it's the next step – nothing stays still. There's always the next demand. Living with us and hearing their stories called us to respond to their pain. We began to understand more and more deeply that our standard of living is complicit with the fact that these people are oppressed. While we profit from the sale of arms to Indonesia, these people are kept annexed and suppressed without self-determination. People are dying in the process.

Our standard of living is built upon the death of these two young men's families. We learnt that and understood it more

FAITH, HOPE AND CHASTITY

deeply. We loved them. They learnt English with us and their personalities broke out. Families opened up to them; people were moved and touched by them. They came to celebrate Lent the following year, in '97, and on Ash Wednesday I felt deeply privileged that one of them, Moises de Costa, should anoint me with ashes. He came up to me to be anointed but I knelt before him and asked him to anoint me. We are all complicit, the Church, all of us. We need to be converted and that's what the ashes do; Ash Wednesday calls the whole Church to repentance.

That day – Ash Wednesday – we went down to the Department of Trade and Industry in Liverpool, which at that time was occupied by some of the Catholic Worker group. I took the ashes I'd been sharing with people all day and anointed the building – the inside of the offices, really. I got expelled for that. Then on each Monday of Lent we travelled with the Timorese young men to the gates of the factory, where they gave out leaflets and pleaded with the workers to think the issues through. Conversion had happened to us. We hoped it might happen to the workers. Could we be exposed to the other end of this arms race chain? The disturbing gift of being evangelized by the poor was being offered to those in the arms trade.

We planned to take our new life, which came from being evangelized by the poor, into the factory and Easter was the right time to do it. This new life included knowledge of our own complicity, and knowledge that a wholeness was only possible through working in solidarity with the oppressed. We went to the factory in the early hours of Easter Monday morning, hoping we might just take them by surprise. At dawn we read Gospel stories inside the aircraft factory; we took our experience into the factory and offered it to BAe as a chance for reflection and a new way of seeing things.

It was a prophetic action but I mean, God help us, compared to the women's action of January '96, it was completely different. Theirs was a proper 'Ploughshares' action – going to a weapon and beating it in an attempt to say, 'This is what Isaiah and the Bible calls us to do, to beat weapons into ploughshares.' What we were doing was something very timid and thin, but it was powerful to us and we wanted to take it to anyone who'd notice – but particularly to the factory. We'd been to the Department of Trade and Industry; we'd written to MPs. This was kind of another action: to go inside the factory gate, knowing it would cause some kind of disturbance.

Eight of us climbed a fence, supported by a bunch of friends. We had a mobile phone which alerted people back in Liverpool to put out fresh press releases as the action took place. We got into the British and Portuguese press, and we were on Free Radio East Timor by lunchtime that day. The Timorese men, they reported, had entered a factory with a priest – an aircraft factory which sent out Hawks that drove over their huts and killed their families.

Technically the case against us was proven by the magistrates as we went to court some months later, in August. At the end of two days' trial, we told our stories. In court, Timorese people who spoke in broken English put questions to BAe employees – public relations people, legal people and security people, together with the slickest and most competent of BAe workers who had been giving evidence that day and who knew how to fend off every question. But one particular moment summed it all up. One of the Timorese young men, Moises de Costa, said: 'Excuse me, sir, but how would *you* feel if you knew the Hawk jets coming out of this factory were terrorizing *your* family and were dropping napalm on *your* family?' And the guy looked around the room, and all his confidence was lost, and he searched for help from the magistrates, from the clerk of the court, from his friends at the back of the room, and he looked back at Costa and he said, 'I wouldn't like it.' To get to that moment was very important. Third World people spoke first-hand to people who get advantage out of the arms trade, so that the consequences of the arms trade are made clear. It happened that day in court.

Our standard of living is built upon the death, oppression and starvation *tonight* of people in other parts of the world. We're alert to that connection and we live with the unease of it, as our bishops have called us to live with the unease of the arms trade. Sometimes people have asked me to do work that isn't parish work but I have to refuse, I can't do that. I would be like a balloon without air in it. I need the community. I've always understood my priesthood in terms of the parish priest and his love for the community. Both Paul VI and John Paul II call local communities to be people not just of values and fine words, but of action and reflection, people who would be converted by their action. I believe I am the most orthodox priest you've ever met. I believe that very much.

I'm driven by what I know is right. I don't believe I'm worthy of what I'm driven by. I know I'm clumsy. I know I'm half-hearted. I know I lack courage. I know that I only do it when supported by others. I'm a weak person who travels in company, driven by the Gospel which is extremely dynamic.

All of this takes place alongside liturgy and the task of involving people in the life of the parish – getting more people to be readers and eucharistic ministers. I encourage people to take responsibility and overcome their fears and inhibitions about things. I am calling people beyond their fears and natural reluctance into confidence and competence, so that faith-sharing and reflection on the Gospel is actually all in place. And to see a parish buzz at all of those levels, not perfectly, often rising and falling, is for me the local parish at its best and I've loved it and worked at it in every parish I've been in. It's grace, and you can see it happen, day after day after day as you work with people. It's wonderful.

14. Father Michael Seed SA

Fr Michael Seed was born in Manchester in 1957

Father Michael Seed is the priest, beloved of the press, who ushers those of other denominations and increasingly those of influence into the Church – the aristocrats, the parliamentarians, the worthies. The conversion of Ann Widdecombe MP – one of his charges – was such a high-profile event that the chapel in the House of Commons was filled mainly with members of the media. Many in the Church resent this penchant for the powerful and feel he only brings in right-wing people – John Selwyn Gummer MP is already installed and Alan Clark MP is waiting in the wings. The resentment, however, is misplaced, for Fr Michael has also brought over whole congregations of people and not just the odd Conservative MP. As a child Fr Seed grew up in a family hammocked between Tridentine Catholicism at one end and extreme evangelical Protestantism at the other; inevitably he embodies ecumenism, and putting non-Catholics at their ease is his forte.

Adopted as a baby but then orphaned at the age of ten, Fr Michael came over as vulnerable and honest – a man who has made serious and difficult attempts to come to terms with the loss not only of his natural parents but also his adoptive parents. With no innate identity, he has jigsawed one together for himself – searching out and hanging on to scraps of information about his past. Indeed, throughout his troubled teenage years he only just found the will to hang on to life itself. Even now, he says, he makes a positive decision every day to choose life and not death. The story of his childhood and the circumstances around his conversion to Catholicism make for remarkable reading.

I was born 42 years ago in Manchester to a single mother – I never knew who my father was. At the age of one I was adopted when my mother, I'm told, was still very young – a lot of these things I found out much later when I was 15 or 16. She'd taken me to the Catholic Children's Society of Salford Diocese when I was about six months old and handed me over to a Sister who is still around, called Sister Philomena. I actually met Sister Philomena when I was about 18 and found out a lot about my background then which was very interesting.

So my mother placed me for adoption. We think she was from Ireland, we don't know. She could have got pregnant in Ireland and come over here because we're talking about 1957, when things were not quite as they are now for single mothers in Ireland. I know the name of my natural mother – it was Marie Godwin, so I was baptized Stephen Wayne Godwin. As I grew up I was always curious as to why I had such a long name, because my adopted parents were Joseph and Lillian Seed which is my legal name. I was given the name Michael and then I was given the name Joseph, because of my adopted father. So I was Michael Joseph Stephen Wayne Seed. I always wondered why I had all these names; it was only at the age of 15 that I found out, when the headmaster of my school told me.

I'm not one of those people who is obsessed with adoption, but it would be good to meet my real mother; if she's still alive now she may well be only 59 or 60. At the same time I can understand all the reasons why not to meet her – she could have got married again, had other children, maybe not even told her husband or anything – it's all very difficult if someone shows up.

I always refer to my late adoptive parents as my mother and father. We lived in a very poor area of Manchester; my father was a prison warden at Strangeways prison and my mother ran a little confectionery shop, which ended up being demolished since it was in a slum area. It meant we had to move out of Manchester to Bolton in Lancashire, in order to live with my adoptive grandmother on my mother's side. She was in the Salvation Army and so was my mother, but she became a Catholic in 1942 when she married my father. In those days you really had to.

So we moved to Bolton because we were effectively homeless. My father was by now working for a telephone company, so he continued to commute from Bolton to Manchester. My mother, meanwhile, got depressed and started taking heavy tranquillizers. She was totally depressed and committed suicide one Saturday morning on a railway track just near where we lived. I was eight at the time.

My mother was a very beautiful lady – very beautiful indeed. I have memories of other men being around – friends of hers. I don't know whether my father ever knew. They weren't relationships exactly, but people definitely took an interest in her. I remember going out with her and another man in a nice car – I think it was a Jaguar and I remember thinking that it was very different to how we lived and I always wondered where my father was. I was five then, five or six.

Just after my mother's suicide, my mother's father died. He was a lollipop man – children's crossings. He was also a helper at the local cinema, which is why I was so conscious of the Saturday morning when she killed herself – because it was on Saturday mornings that I would go with my grandfather to the Odeon cinema in the centre of Bolton. We'd always watch Laurel and Hardy. So I remember it very profoundly; I would have been preparing to go to the cinema.

I was in the kitchen playing at the time. A knock came at the back door from this lady who said to my grandfather that he'd better come quickly. That was all. My grandfather and father went running out to the scene leaving me with my grandmother. I felt confused because I didn't know she was dead at that point. They just said, 'It's Lillian – come quickly, something very bad has happened.' So I wasn't sure, but I suspected. Even then I sensed she must have died or something very drastic must have happened.

From that moment on I shut off; I just went very odd, very withdrawn. I withdrew because it was just all too shocking, especially because it happened under the railway bridge that I had to cross every morning to go to school. I also had to cope with the notoriety. In those days things like that didn't happen very often; this was 1965. We were in a little village in Bolton and so it got into the newspaper and word spread around and I just wanted to hide; I wanted to run away.

So it was all a very tragic beginning. My grandmother was in her seventies at this point and effectively became my mother.

She died ten years ago in her nineties, having become a Catholic a few years before her death when Bishop Gordon Wheeler was very instrumental in her reception into the Catholic Church. Soon after this I was taken away from Bolton by my father who dumped me in Liverpool with his mother and sister – my aunt Sheila who lived at home and is still alive now. His father was already dead. I then went to school in Liverpool for a year and a half, which was a total disruption because it meant leaving a little world in which I was reasonably settled. I'd been to school in Manchester for one or two years until the shop was sold, then in Bolton with my grandmother for one or two years, and now Liverpool for one or two years. My father then brought me *back* to Bolton where he dumped me with my grandmother again, who was by that stage on her own. I didn't see him at all after that and he died a year later from a brain tumour. I was by now ten years old.

I was so numbed by my mother's death, then my grandfather's death, and then all this moving around that my father's death didn't really register. After that I was yet again whisked away, this time to live in Stockport with my Bolton grandmother's adopted son. She only had one natural child, my adoptive mother, but she also adopted a boy called Leslie who I call my uncle. I stayed with them for two or three months before returning to Bolton and that helped a little bit.

At the point of my father's death Bolton Social Services intervened immediately. My legal guardians were now number one, my grandmother, and number two, her adopted son Leslie. When I returned to Bolton I went back into my little primary school and eventually failed my 11-plus … naturally, because I sat there and didn't do anything. I couldn't read or write until I was 13.

I was taken to see a child psychiatrist every week because emotionally I was totally withdrawn, and academically I didn't do anything. The therapy was never private; my grandmother was always there. It was odd. We're going back to the therapy of 1963; it wouldn't happen that way today. I would go to this very formal lady who was more like a magistrate than a psychiatrist. She was very funny with these rather frightening Dame Edna Everage glasses. In fact she looked like Dame Edna, except that she was serious. One went to make an account of oneself for not being able to read and write; it was Dickensian.

In terms of religion, I was raised Tridentine Catholic in the morning and Salvation Army in the evening. I was baptized a Catholic by my real mother in the Church of the Holy Name in Manchester – at that time a big Jesuit Church. And the Seeds, who adopted me, were also Catholic although my adopted mother, of course, had been raised in the Salvation Army. I was considered a Catholic because I went to the Catholic primary school, so the curates used to visit me; I remember hiding from them behind the curtains.

My grandmother tolerated this Catholicism. She was very devout and very saintly, a very holy woman indeed. She said her morning prayer and evening prayer. And all her music, all her records were evangelical – Billy Graham and the evangelical Baptist singers of the forties, fifties and sixties. It was a very religious household with Bible tracts on the walls; it was very spiritual.

In the evenings there was a Salvation Army service but in the mornings a Latin Mass. Sometimes I wouldn't go to Mass; I would just stand outside. Or I'd go on my bicycle with these friends of mine and we'd ride round the park. I was only seven or eight but you didn't need adults with you in those days. We were free to go as we pleased; nobody took us to Mass. Sometimes we went to Mass in the church, and sometimes we just said we went there – which we did. We just didn't go to Mass. It was boring and it was terrifying – to me as a child it was absolutely terrifying. I remember singing in the choir and being an altar boy, and finding the priests frightening and pompous. The priesthood in those days was a total turn-off; I saw them as ferocious inquisitors. How dare they come and bang on the door to see where I was! I didn't like that, they were like policemen. So my early memories are of priests as inquisitors. Moreover, as my Salvation Army religious development began I was told that Catholicism was a religion of fear, which of course was confirmed to me in childhood.

So my first memories of Catholicism and the priesthood are of great fear and a very strange language, because Latin meant nothing to me. The Salvation Army, on the other hand, had a band and was exciting. I remember ridiculous scenarios of having my first Holy Communion and wearing funny little clothes. Rosary beads were given to me, along with little medals and a white missal, and I remember taking all this stuff with me to the

FAITH, HOPE AND CHASTITY

Salvation Army in the evening. I thought they were religious things so I might as well take them there. It was very odd and very strange to see the contrast between them.

To have had such extreme ecumenical experiences at that age is fascinating. Mind you, the Salvation Army for me as a child was equally frightening because the ministers wore uniforms. My father also had a uniform because he was a prison warden, and the prison warden uniform and the Salvation Army uniform are not that different. So really I equated religion as on being a par with Sir Oswald Mosley's Blackshirts! But what I did find fun was the fact they had tambourines and bands and they were very lively; it wasn't too militaristic. But both experiences for me were very fundamentalist and made me very frightened. I remember the Salvation Army had a 'mercy bench'. We were all called out to go and kneel at this mercy bench so as to be saved, to be born again, to give our lives to Christ. It was done at every service.

Those services were very similar to Billy Graham's rallies. In 1989 I was greatly involved with Billy Graham's mission to London in Earls Court; I talked Cardinal Hume into going. It was a great ecumenical breakthrough, not just because Catholics were involved but because all the other clergy from the Protestant Churches agreed to this. I was given the cards of all the Catholics who went forward – thousands of them. There was an agreement that the people who went forward would be offered contact with a minister of their own denomination. I discovered several nuns and a few seminarians! I even discovered the sacristan of a leading church in London, which is very funny. I ended up with about 5,000 Catholic forms which I then had to distribute to the relevant parish priests. Each priest was contacted by the Cardinal. 'Dear Father,' he wrote, 'these people are in need of help ... would you please call on them ...' But I had no idea what to do with these nuns and seminarians. I didn't want to tell their superiors they'd been converted!

The religious figures of my childhood were frightening but they were also commanding. Children naturally look up in awe and can be easily led, so these great commanding figures also gave me strength. If one was commanded to believe in God or commanded to believe in life after death, one did. I was commanded to, so I did. It stopped me from thinking for a little while but I didn't mind.

I was so 'out of it' – sociologically and psychologically – that this religious world was like a little haven. Even though I found the churches frightening and terrifying, going to them was almost addictive. They were absolutist and I suppose in a very odd way that must have affected me in terms of absolutes today. If people ask me whether I believe in the Resurrection ... well, 'Yes,' I say, 'I do.' I can't theologically explain it but I do. Or what about the Ascension, they say. Well yes, again I do believe in it. Whether it's because I'm just obedient or because it's been drummed into me, or whether it's because I really understand it, I don't know.

In 1969 I went to a brand new school that had just been built called Knowle View School in Rochdale. It was a school for 'maladjusted' children – a special school. Today we wouldn't use those terms, but they did in 1969. It was part boarding, part children's home and was filled with some nice children and some really wacky children. Some had been abused, others were a bit mad, others were thieves. In those days I don't think people quite knew what to do with children like that.

I was very attracted by the school's great fields and its white colours – it was an ultra-modern building. It seemed like a fun place and it got me away. I was then 12 and I'd had just one year in a dreadful Catholic secondary school. It was absolutely horrible, with lots of bullying because the boys who remembered me from the age of six or seven were there. My parents were both dead but I still remember inventing all sorts of jobs for my father. Pretending they weren't dead was a form of denial because one wanted to fit in or appear normal with the other children, so I just made up jobs for my father.

It was a breath of fresh air when I arrived at the school because all the other children were similar to myself, so I stayed there for four years. Religiously, it was interesting because every month when I came home to stay with my grandmother we went to a Baptist church, since I had an uncle by affection there who was a travelling evangelist like Billy Graham. He was preaching in this little very independent Baptist church. It was actually called the 'Strict and Particular Baptist Church' and was a member of the Fellowship of Independent Evangelical Churches (FIEC), which still exists today.

FAITH, HOPE AND CHASTITY

We first went to this church when the man I call my uncle was preaching. He was quite a noted evangelist – a lovely man called Harold Watson, Pastor Harold Watson. Baptists practise baptism by total immersion but he only believed in baptism by the Holy Spirit. But he was such a holy man that they employed him anyway as a Baptist minister, and whenever they needed to do a baptism they would simply bring in somebody else and he'd preach at it. So I went there for a while and quite liked it. It was a very intimate little church and I liked the service; people made us feel welcome. I didn't know much about the theology, I just went there – every month for four years. It was also known as Bethel Church, Bolton and was very extreme. They regarded the Baptist Union of Great Britain as unsound – heretical. In our theology Methodists were grossly unsound and the Church of England largely heretical; they were not saved. And Roman Catholics were a cult and were damned – they were of the devil. I remember the priest coming to visit us when I was seven or eight and thinking as I hid behind the curtains, 'Oh yes, I can understand that.'

We had to convert Catholics as well as people in general at Sunday football matches; some of the earliest memories I have are of wandering outside football stadiums and handing out Bible tracts to convert the crowds. I have even earlier memories of going in to pubs and selling *The War Cry* as a Salvationist. The Salvation Army are much kinder and softer in terms of their theology; they would never have made such attacks on Catholicism. That's why Cardinal Manning could be such good friends with General Booth. They united in a Temperance League against alcohol because they knew it was keeping the poor in poverty.

The extreme Baptists saw Catholicism and the whole institution of the Church as erroneous. They respected the office of St Peter but they did not believe there could be a second or a third Pope, the idea of apostolic succession was just not on. The sacraments and the real presence of Christ in the Eucharist were anathema to them – they couldn't cope with the sacraments. We were fundamentalist with respect to the Gospel. We believed you first had to receive the call and understand Christ before you were baptized and then you had to make your public testimony before the community. You make your testimony, then you're baptized and then you're saved. So theologically it all made sense to me. At that point, aged about 13, Catholicism for me was deeply erroneous and theologically unsound. However, I wasn't anti-Catholic. I was simply conscious that I was a Christian and was more familiar with Baptism.

I heard some of the finest preachers – Ian Paisley would drop to his knees in awe if he heard those names. Dr Martin Lloyd Jones was at that point the most eminent evangelical preacher in Britain, if not the world. He would have been on a par with Billy Graham in terms of the British Isles. We would have supper with him, my grandmother and I, since he had to be accommodated overnight, and I remember at the age of 14 or 15 going to great Saturday night evangelical rallies. It was fascinating listening to them.

I used to read a lot of little Bible tracts, the type of thing that you get on Victoria Street converting you – today they come from Westminster Chapel. Then at the age of 15 I was baptized by total immersion, which was frightening because the tank was very cold. I made my testimony and everything. It was in Farnworth Baptist Church and I was anxious for weeks beforehand. I worried about whether I was really converted. Am I really a Christian, am I damned and am I going to go to Hell? Am I saved? How do I know I'm saved? I asked all these questions and was terrified about it. I made this very little testimony, I didn't know what I was saying really. I think I wrote little notes down, only little things. I said them out loud and then I got baptized and that was it. I remember not feeling totally comfortable at that baptism.

I wanted to go to Emmanuel Bible College when I was 17 years old and become a minister of the Church. But I was still only 16 so I got my first job with Bolton Social Services. I was actually in care with them but at the same time was employed by them. I worked in a home for elderly and mentally ill people until I was 18, which was fascinating. I encountered a rag-and-bone man there who was one of the residents of the hall, a crazy person. He always used to wear white opera gloves to eat. He wouldn't wash his hands, he'd put on white opera gloves. I was making his supper one night and he got so hungry that he ate the goldfish – like sardines. He made himself toast and put them on – absolutely true. I don't know how the scene happened but the

FAITH, HOPE AND CHASTITY

kitchen had these little goldfish things around and they weren't there when I came back – they were gone via his plate. The reason he got so hungry was that I was reading a copy of the *Salford Catholic Directory* which he'd brought in. I was very interested in anything religious so I read this. By that point I was a deeply committed Baptist and was preparing to go to the Bible college, but I just saw this *Salford Catholic Directory*, and it was the first time I'd ever brought myself back to thinking about Catholicism because it was all meant to be so evil.

Prior to this, an Anglican priest who worked with us in the boarding school had taken a particular interest in me when I was about 13, and had started to challenge me on my religious views. He was Anglo-Catholic and was amused by me. I was like a little Dr Paisley. It was so funny, I was absolutely Protestant. He smoked and drank – both of those were meant to be evil – and he went to the theatre and cinema – they were evil too. So he really amused me too, but he also changed me by telling me to read. By the age of 13 or 14 I had learnt to read but was reading weird things like Darwin's *Origin of Species*, which I thought was evil. We believed in Adam and Eve and that was it and today, when people ask me whether I believe Adam and Eve existed, I still say, 'Well yes, it's quite possible.' We can believe in evolution and we can believe in Adam and Eve. Adam and Eve could take place in one day while evolution could take place in ten million years. I am still slightly sympathetic to people who have these very fundamentalist views. I can't say it's impossible. This Anglo-Catholic priest used to challenge me on this type of stuff so I then read philosophy – weird things that people wouldn't normally read at that age: Wittgenstein, Nietzsche, Kierkegaard, Hegel, Bertrand Russell, Oscar Wilde. He made me read *The Importance of Being Earnest*, because that sent up religion a little bit. I also read Shakespeare and Dickens; I just read anything I wanted.

I've hardly done any science in my life, and I've never done maths or biology. In fact I would say that 75 per cent of one's normal education I don't have. I am seriously flawed academically but I loved reading, so I had the luxury from the age of 13 to 16 of reading what most children wouldn't read – mostly set by this Anglican chaplain. I even read Marx and Hitler's *Mein Kampf*!

I also developed a fascination with Communism, which was another thing that made me slightly anti-Catholic; I thought of it as being imperialist by nature. Moreover, the Baptists tended to be much more working class than the Anglicans; the nonconformist tradition is often from the poorer section. Little did I know that Communism and Catholicism actually go hand-in-hand, to the extent that there is a great sense of equality within Catholicism; that's how I can be happy as a Catholic today. But I always describe myself as an uncomfortable Catholic; at times I love Catholicism but at other times I absolutely hate it and frequently challenge it.

If people are interested in Catholicism, I never sell it to them. In fact, in many ways I do the opposite, which they probably find attractive because what I communicate to them is Christianity, it's not Catholicism at all. I leave it up to them to work out where they feel comfortable in Christianity, in faith. But for me the Catholic Church is the Church of essence – origin and essence – and the other Churches are part of us. Catholicism is the Universal Christian Church and that's all; it is the Christian Church. Denominationalism I don't understand. What I do know is that the other denominations are often the result of our own sin and pride and arrogance; they exist because of our theological error and unwillingness to learn.

I sometimes find the General Synod concept of the Church of England attractive, and yet sometimes I hate it because of the politics. I have a bit of involvement with parliamentary figures and I see how quickly people can switch for their own aims. Democracy as worked out in the General Synod can have its problems. I always remember Archbishop Runcie saying how the Anglican Communion prides itself on its diversity. But at what point does diversity become so diverse as to be meaningless? There's been a move within the Anglican community to make the profile of the office of the Archbishop of Canterbury much more that of a world leader. I just wonder if moving into this greater form of authoritative governors is the way we should be going.

It was after I'd read all those books as a child that I knew I couldn't be a Baptist minister. My 'Strict and Particular' church was becoming too exclusive for me. So I went to a local Anglican vicar who knew I'd been a Catholic and who proceeded to give me a course of instruction in all the differences between Catholicism and Anglicanism – incredibly slanted to his stance of course, which was evangelical Protestant Anglicanism. I didn't want to be received into the Anglican Church, but I went ahead with it anyway because I didn't want to let him down.

A week later I went over the road into a Catholic Church and that's what converted me on the spot. It was an evening Mass and I was 18. I went into this church and there was this old, grumpy priest. He said Mass with his back to the people; I think it might even have been in Latin then, even though this was 1974. Half the congregation were drunk; the pub was next door and the church reeked of alcohol. The other half were saying the rosary. I didn't know what they were doing; they were all mumbling little things and not paying any attention. No hymns, a horrible sermon, incense and this grumpy priest telling everybody off. I saw all this and suddenly said to myself, 'This is the Church,' because it was full of sinners – they were all sinners in there.

They drank alcohol – 'That's interesting,' I thought, 'So why do they come to church?' I don't know ... it was just so messy, dirty and horrible and all my other experiences had been so clean. It had all been so clean and perfect; everything was nice, a beautiful welcome. No one got a welcome in this Catholic church. No one bothered me when I came in; nobody handed me anything – no books, no welcome. And nobody paid any attention when I left. It was all so filthy and horrible. Apart from the incense and the alcohol and the rosary there were also the accents: Irish, Italian, Filipino, plus strange people – black people, all different colours of people. It was all so interesting.

That night I rang the doorbell of the parish priest – which you should never do on a Sunday night. He was about 80 and when he answered the door I told him that I'd come from the Anglican church – St Paul's – over the road. I told him that I'd also been at Bethel Church. Can you imagine trying to explain all this to an old priest, a grumpy old priest? I could tell he wanted his supper so he just said, 'What are you?'

'I'm an Anglican,' I said, 'but only just. Before that I was a Baptist at Bethel Church and before that I was a Catholic – baptized and confirmed.'

'You're a Catholic then,' he said, 'you'll be all right.'

'Well, yes,' I said, 'but it would be nice to talk about all this.'

'Oh all right then, you'd better come in.'

He sat me down and said he thought I needed a drink. I'd never tasted alcohol before, never. So he gave me what I think was an enormous gin and campari or something like that. It was very strong and I was knocked out; we may have even had supper.

I went to see him every Sunday night. I'd have another gin and we'd talk. We went through the little Penny Catechism and then I'd have another gin. We just went through it, that was all. Then had more gin. We did! He was such a sweet old priest, but very grumpy to look at and we just talked about anything.

The reason I became a Catholic and the reason I stay a Catholic are very different. I became one because of all the dirtiness and sinfulness; the Catholic Church is able to cope with all that very well. It's sublime. It's saintliness and despair, good and evil – it's the Church, the whole hodgepodge of humanity. It's very similar to the theology of Teilhard de Chardin, which is all about the consecration of the whole universe, the whole of creation. The essence of the Catholic Church – its substance, its foundation – is that it's *the* Christian Church. That's what I believe in.

It might shock people to say this but often, humorously, I think to myself that my concern is not always with remaining a priest but with putting up with the bumpiness and 'blunderliness' of Catholicism itself. What I find difficult is staying a Catholic. I am much happier being a Franciscan, with its great spirit of universal acceptance and its love of all created things. From the age of 14 or 15 I knew that I wanted to be a minister of the Gospel. I was privileged at 14 or 15 to have accepted a lot in terms of spirituality – the existence of God, for example, who I hated and detested for taking away my parents and giving me such a horrible life. At the age of ten I said that I would commit suicide at 13 – I made a private vow. And when I was 13 I made the same vow that I'd die at 16. I had nothing to live for; I just wanted to die.

When I was an evangelical in a congregational-style church we got to choose our clergy. We'd bring them all down – ten of them – and we'd look at their wives as well, and their children if necessary. And the ministers would preach for us and we'd interview them. We had elders and people like that and the whole congregation would listen to them preach and meet them. The Catholic Church is a very clerical domain and the laity are often considered as onlookers. I also find it odd the way we issue edicts and decrees. I know we have to have rules – very much so – because I am an absolutist myself. But it's the way we understand our rules, whether they are imposed on us, or whether there is also some listening – on behalf of the bishops, the priests and the people.

I received the essence of Christianity as an evangelical and I'm still a fundamentalist Christian. The priesthood is not – it might sound shocking – but it's not the be-all and end-all of my existence. Had I not been moved to Catholicism I would still be a minister of the Church. Had I gone to a better church I probably would have been a Baptist minister. So Catholicism has no monopoly on spirituality or salvation, of course not.

I was ordained in America but came straight back to Britain, where for the first five years I was chaplain to Westminster Hospital and also to a school for mentally and physically disabled children. Then the Cardinal asked me if I would be Ecumenical Officer for the diocese of Westminster. In those days, back in 1987, many of the characters I knew in the evangelical world had become quite prominent. So if I wanted to meet the General of the Salvation Army I'd just call my uncle. 'Oh, come along Michael,' he'd say and off I'd go to the General's office. It was the same with many of the other Churches.

I've just turned 42 and my absolutes are less strong than they were. I don't feel any holier or more spiritual since I started practising as a Roman Catholic. I think the experiences I had between the ages of 13 and 18 were very profound and spiritually very helpful and it's those that keep me going, especially the experience of wanting to choose life and not death, of deciding not to end my life at 13 or 16. The priesthood is not something I dwell a lot on, which must sound very odd. It isn't what I am. It also isn't something I simply do because then it would be just like a job, a nine-to-five job. It isn't that. It's part of an overall picture and the more important thing is to choose every day one's reason to live, or, to put it better if that sounds too drastic, understanding the purpose of life each day. It's very similar to the 12 Steps of AA. I know many alcoholics and they all have to make that choice every day. Well, I'm like that.

I do have struggles, I still have all the struggles today; they are not healed at all. I am still going through the struggles of having to choose the positive things of the day. I get very frightened of inadequacy, very frightened indeed, and I think it's only by chance that I've ended up at the Cathedral. The only house my Order owns in the whole of Great Britain is at the very back of the Cathedral. It's circumstantial. If I'd joined any other Order, I wouldn't be attached to the Cathedral.

The Cathedral is a very public place, a very busy place, and I preach my sermons to vast crowds; it can be very stressful. I get stage fright – going out to say the six o'clock Mass in the Cathedral is not easy, not easy at all. I'm always nervous. I'm never relaxed and that's good because it gets one's adrenalin going. I'm never relaxed about it. When I had the six o'clock Mass last Saturday night I knew I had about a thousand people out there and I knew I had to preach. I never use a script, I can't, it has to come out of me – it's got to be natural. I make mistakes in my sermons and my grammar must be dreadful for the hearer. I have all those feelings of fear – fear of the performance. Most of them have to do with vanity because I'm worried about what people will think of me. Sometimes I just want to break down in tears in the middle of the Mass, or I might be feeling a bit depressed or a bit low, but of course I can't break down. But then in normal life you can't either. If you're a teacher you've got to teach your class. If you're a doctor or a surgeon you've got to do that nine o'clock operation. You switch on to what you have to be.

I'm diplomatic with my sermons. I hate shocking people. My great thing is to build on where people are at, and what they have. I have sat through so many damn sermons where priests and theologians are trying to show off their intelligence at the expense of the people. I don't want to be demeaning, but I think many people come to Mass not always for the greatest and most inspiring sermons, but for the mystery, and to be fed sometimes in ways they don't know. A lot of our faith is unspoken and unknown and people come for the mystery. They come to be told the story and in my opinion that should never change. It's a very simple story and the ceremony of the Mass is a perfect format for it.

I feel content. I've been very blessed ever since the age of seven or eight with families that have adopted me in childhood. Even nowadays I have very good friends and that does help. But still one can't help but feel lonely – you do, I do. But not to the point of despair, no. It's the nature of the life I chose. I would say even if I were in another life, I would probably have the same feelings; therefore it's as well that I have chosen to be a priest.

The way one lives is normal, so for me I've had a normal upbringing; it's other people who are interested in it. It's only in the last ten years – since all these damn converts – that I've started talking about it. Had I not received these converts into the Church nobody would be interested.

The rewards I think I've experienced are identification with people. I think to myself, 'Today I've met someone who is much worse off than I am.' Solidarity and identification are some of the only consolations I have. The beauty of entering into people's lives – the joy and the sadness. It's normality, consistency and balance. It's identification. With a funeral or a marriage or a new baby one enters into humanity. There's a grimness to it as well, but then there's a lot of grimness in life. Maybe I'm too grim. I don't think I'm a depressive; I turn tragic things into funniness sometimes, my own life – I do often make fun of it. I ridicule it, but it isn't as sad as people think. I don't think I've had a sad existence. To me it's totally normal. People ask me, 'Did you want brothers and sisters?' Or they say, 'Would you like a mother and father?' and I say, 'Well, it could have been nice, but I don't know.' I'm quite happy and contented because I've developed many mothers and fathers. I don't feel deprived; I think that's what I'm trying to say.

15. Brother Stephen de Kerdrel OFMCap

*Br Stephen de Kerdrel was born in Beda, Holland
in 1953 to French/British parents*

It has always struck me that some priests actually *look* holy.
Br Stephen de Kerdrel is without doubt one of these; in fact he is
the most holy-looking priest I have ever come across. Perhaps
this is something he cultivates; his long hair and flowing beard
certainly remind one of Jesus – or maybe John the Baptist. But a
look in the eyes cannot be cultivated, nor a manner so alive with
energy that it verges on mania. Like other holy people I have
met in my life, Br Stephen appears at some level 'transparent',
receiving and transmitting through his very being the love of
God. His presence is not thick and blocked and corpulent but
rather light and fluid and bubbling over with joy.

Such people are contagious – one wants to be with them, or at
least hang on to the memory of their face and words for as long
as possible. But I could also imagine Br Stephen suffering from
some kind of mental instability – perhaps manic depression –
were it not for the fact that he lives in a religious Order as one
of the Franciscan Capuchins. His mental agility and emotional
effervescence are focused and anchored in the strict rule of
St Francis of Assisi and the result is explosive – an eruption
of sheer creativity.

Br Stephen has always wanted to be a saint. As a child he was
given model altars with tabernacles which he would carefully
open; friends even nicknamed him 'Saint'. He was born in Holland but brought up in England from the age of two – his family,
Anglo-French and aristocratic – were Catholic but not particularly 'churchy'. His grandmother was an opera singer and his

mother a dancer with the Ballet Rambert. His father received the MC for his services in the French army; however, as recounted by Br Stephen, he was a crook who had physical but not moral courage and was later convicted for embezzlement. For all his laughter, the life of Br Stephen has not been easy. The child of divorced parents, he lost his brother to Aids – a death which caused him great suffering and which, he says, changed his faith for ever. There is also the question of Br Stephen's 'Damascus' style conversion and his apocalyptic belief in the end of Western civilization: these are just some of the elements which make up a truly mesmerizing man.

I was a supposedly 'good' Catholic compared to most of my contemporaries at school – I mean, I was very proper. I think on the whole I would have been considered exemplary – I was a virgin and still am – I'm a rarity these days, you know. But I always seemed to have a reputation for being good, which surprises me because I'm a dreadful gossip. I used to be amazed at school because I was considered really very eccentric and so I never got bullied, never; the bullies used to come and look at me as if I was a monkey in a cage. I thought they were being nice. I remember, years later a great school friend of mine went up to one of these famous school bullies at a diplomatic cocktail party and really let this man have it. I didn't even know this chap had been a bully; I had no idea. I was always a bit of a dreamer.

I always felt called to preach, probably because I'm an incorrigible chatterbox. I was fascinated by the poverty of St Francis of Assisi, but a child of 11 can't really take it all in so from about the age of 13 my vocation petered away and went into cold storage. I took a year off after school because I thought that I might want to be an opera singer. I had musical contacts that people would kill for. I knew Benjamin Britten, Peter Pears and Placido Domingo, who I met in 1979. Having lived in Aldeburgh I knew Britten and Pears because we were brought up with them; I used to sit on Ben's knee as a little boy and draw on his manuscript paper. But when I went to the famous Otakar Kraus, who was a Czech Jewish baritone and a very fine singer, he said I didn't have a hope in hell. 'Go and be a teacher,' he said. 'You could become a head teacher, but you won't become a great singer.' And he was right. What he detected was nothing to do with the voice, it was my lack of ambition.

So I went to Sheffield University to study Mediaeval and Ancient History and in 1973 nearly had a nervous breakdown. I think it was because I was burning the candle at both ends, going to bed at three and getting up at seven. And that coincided with my eldest brother Anthony going bankrupt, so it was all terribly unfortunate. He used to run a well-known gallery in London called 'Situation' which was very much the place to go in the early seventies.

Then in late 1974 I began to think a bit more about my vocation and I said to my mother, 'I wonder why Our Lady doesn't appear so much these days?' Whereupon, whatever book I picked up, it was about Marian Apparitions. Then in May of 1975 something extraordinary happened to me. I had a conversion experience – in the authentic mediaeval sense of really accepting Christ as Lord of my life. It was a week in which suddenly everything changed. I'd been a very liberal Catholic. I didn't do anything particularly wrong but I was quite happy for everyone to sleep together before they got married – all the kind of liberal stuff that's still quite popular today. And then, as a result of what I can only describe as the direct intervention of the Holy Spirit, everything changed. Suddenly, I saw a completely different thing and that liberal, worldly view went out of the window.

I suddenly found that my conversion experience wasn't simply on the level of the emotions. Conversion isn't. On the intellectual level as well, I found that suddenly everything was just completely reversed. Prior to this conversion I would have said that Paul VI was, you know, a doddery old fool and that he was wrong about *Humanae Vitae*. And then suddenly I realized that I was wrong and he was right, that everything had just suddenly changed and that life had become completely different. There was a radical shift. I used to say that the Church should validate homosexual relationships – I actually preached it in our chaplaincy chapel – also that it was all right to live together and that contraception was all right. I was never keen on abortion; I drew the line there. But I thought as long as it didn't hurt anyone it was all right. The conversion wasn't anything I did. It was done to me. It makes absolutely no sense but

FAITH, HOPE AND CHASTITY

I can only describe that week 22 years ago in May as like exploding fireworks – or walking on air. And I can't tell you why I use those metaphors or similes or whatever. It was just extraordinary.

Then suddenly I found myself engaged, which was odd because I wasn't in love. On reflection I realized that I had fallen in love with the idea of being in love. This great friend of mine, Barbara Wysoki, returned from a year in Spain as part of her English and Spanish degree. Absence had indeed made the heart grow fonder, and suddenly I found myself proposing to her and strangely she accepted. As soon as I'd done it, I knew it was wrong; meanwhile the religious vocation just erupted. I remember going into Westminster Cathedral and I said, 'Lord, I've not got the courage to break this one off. You'd better make Barbara do it.' And sure enough, she did. She's now very happily married with three children. I realized that the Lord did hear my prayers and then I decided I must do something about it.

A priest called Jeremy Davis became my confessor and first spiritual director, and we had a sort of tug of war because I said I thought I was meant to be an opera singer. We had this tussle over whether or not I had a vocation, and I suppose I would describe the vocation as almost like being in love. I wanted it but at the same time didn't want it. I finally applied to the Capuchins in 1978 and Stephen Innes, the novice master, said to me, 'You have got a vocation but it's not in a very healthy state. I'd go away for a little while.' Which I did.

I think I was drawn to the Capuchins rather than the Friars Conventual because there's a kind of homeliness about them, a kind of down-to-earth quality and approachability. Not that I'd really met many friars, but when I did meet them I found them very approachable men. The Order was semi-contemplative; someone described them as being like the Staretz, the Russian hermits. There was something of a magetism about them. The whole thing of reconciling and healing appealed to me, almost, I suppose, more than preaching. I could only enunciate this later on, in retrospect, but there was a kind of warmth, a sunny quality.

When I finally joined the postulancy in 1981 I remember sitting in the refectory at Pantasaph Friary thinking I had come home. There was a sense that I was now in the right place, and I've felt that ever since.

One of the biggest obstacles in my life has been that by nature I'm prone to considerable anxiety, which probably has something to do with my childhood. I was a great worrier which was allied to a very happy temperament. I mean, I've not been unhappy – I've had sufferings in my life, but that's not the same thing. But I think we were all brought up with that legalistic notion that if you kept all the rules perfectly and didn't put a foot wrong you'd get to heaven fast. The Church was still rather affected by Jansenism – the Catholic form of Calvinism whereby the few will be saved and the majority damned – and also Pelagianism whereby you could get to heaven on your own efforts as opposed to everything depending on grace. I then began to realize, to use the term of one of our priors, that I had to 'let go and let God' ... let go of all my worries and anxieties about life. When I was being brought up it was all very much sin, though as my mother was a convert we didn't have that rather gloomy view of things. I remember once when I was about eight, my mother said, 'Oh, a lie is a mortal sin, Stephen.' I was so shocked – she must have had a rather Lutheran perspective – that I burst into tears and was inconsolable. My father said, 'Oh, a lie isn't a mortal sin.' Well, as he'd spent his life lying I suppose he had a vested interest. But anyway the Order appealed to me – trying to live the vocation of loving one's brothers, serving whoever one meets and loving them, and in my case bridling my tongue.

By nature I'm hypercritical, which sometimes surprises people because I'm by no means as critical as I used to be, but I was always very demanding. It's always the way. One's demanding of other people and forgets to be demanding with oneself. St John of the Cross says, 'To curb your tongue for half an hour is better than a day on bread and water.' And he's right, you know. I think with the Franciscan calling we seem to fail so lamentably these days compared to the early days of Francis. Francis called us to be brothers to one another. He says of the friars that a brother should have a spiritual love for his brother which is greater than a mother's love. And he's very strong on that. So I really did – although I'm sure I didn't do it very well – try to serve the brothers as best I could when I was studying.

I realized in 1983, quite early on in my religious life, that I had a special work to do regarding peace and reconciliation and that's never left me, which is not odd because that's what Francis was like. But it hit me in a very powerful way. Ever since then, that's been another guiding star in my life, greatly aided by St Francis de Sales who was known for winning people over with his great gentleness. I've tried to model myself on him because by nature I have a fiery and explosive temper and a tendency to hysteria under stress, so I've needed that kind of Savoyard phlegm.

People find me joyful and happy, but that doesn't mean to say that I don't have these real faults. I mean, I will sort of explode. I once remember a fellow friar said to me something very stern and he was right. He said, 'I've never met such an egocentric person in all my life.' But I think he didn't realize he was inspired by the Holy Spirit to cut me down to size. I don't know what I was saying – I was obviously bragging about something.

Celibacy has been a constant struggle, but it's interesting, people talk a lot about celibacy and sexuality and all these things, but chastity, which is consecrated love, they say very little about. You have to make up your mind that you are going to love God in the way that he wants you to and then just get on with it. And of course there are all the temptations and everything, but I'm reminded of Gertrude the Great when Christ said to her, 'Who do you love most in your father's castle, the hunting dogs or the lapdogs? The lapdogs stay at home and never get dirty. The hunting dogs go out and get bruised and bloodied and covered with mud.' And she said she preferred the hunting dogs. So I think we become holy with the struggles; we don't become holy in a perfect world where everything's marvellous. With so many priests and religious rushing off and getting married, I often say to people that the heroic vocation in the Church is not priesthood but marriage, because a priest or a religious can always go into his or her own room at night and close the door and be by themselves. But if you're married it's very difficult. Marriage requires continual patience and charity and availability. The priest can quite easily hide if he wants. So I've always thought that this is what I'm called to and I'm going to get on with it to the best of my ability, because it isn't at the end of the day anything to do with Stephen de Kerdrel, or whether he's good, bad or indifferent. This is what I'm called to and everything else fits into place.

Francis of Assisi was the troubadour for Christ. He had a wonderful way of taking society and transforming it. He walked beside people, not like the Church today. The Church has become terribly professional; people are always rushing off to meetings. Everything is meetings or seminars when really it is about the 'anawim', or 'little ones' of the Old Testament – the unimportant people.

At one time I used to like people like Elijah and Amos and Moses, the great prophets – I thought what wonderful people they all were. But now I would prefer to be with Ruth and Boaz or Tobias, Tobit, Hannah, Elizabeth and Zachariah, and, as I was saying to someone the other day, even Joseph and Mary. 'Gosh,' I thought, 'one's pitching one's sights a bit high!' There's nothing I like better by nature than the limelight, playing to the gallery – but the idea now is that as I progress in my religious life, to some extent I'm preferring to back away from things, to be in the background, and to serve people.

The transition from being a layman to being a friar has felt very natural. I'm not saying it's been easy, but it's been natural. My grandmother prayed for a priest in the family and I feel that I didn't have a lot of say in it; it was already mapped out. I could have absolutely rejected it but I would have had to work hard; in some ways it's the most natural thing in the world for me. When I look at some of my fellow friars and priests who have had tremendous struggles and who have been heroic, I ask myself, 'Well, what have I done?' ... very little. It's been easy, not that I haven't experienced suffering.

In 1994 I was having an awful lot of extra work put on me; I was very tired and drained so I went away for a retreat, and during the first and second nights there I had the most appalling panic attacks that I've ever had in my life. I felt listless, as though everything was closing in on me. I really thought I was going to die; it was frightful.

I woke the guardian at our friary and told him and he said, 'Well, you look all right to me!' It was after this that my brother Jeremy rang me up and said, 'You know the pneumonia I had? It was more than pneumonia.' Until then I had never clicked. The cousins had tumbled to it but the immediate family hadn't. So I said, 'Well, you've got Aids, haven't you?' And he said, 'In the

States they call it Aids, but here, you know ... ' and he tried to say that in Britain they needed more evidence before saying it was full-blown Aids. Of course he was trying to avoid the terrible truth, namely that he was under a death sentence. After that it was a downhill trek; he got worse and worse – one step forward, two steps back.

In 1995 my brother died of Aids. He was gay but he'd been faithful to one partner for years. In 1987 I said to him, 'Have you ever gone for one of these tests?' and he said, 'Oh no, there wouldn't be any point.' So I just accepted that he knew what he was talking about, little realizing that even then he knew he had HIV. He just lied to me.

It wasn't until the final weeks of his life that I began to understand the nature of the problem between my brother and I. It wasn't with what he was doing, although from a moral point of view I would say no, they shouldn't have been doing that. The problem had been that he was an introvert born into a family of extroverts. How could the poor man survive? He was living a different life. And I suddenly realized in those final weeks that I had made – that we'd all made – a dreadful mistake. I used to think I didn't love him. He seemed to be too distant; I was always making the effort and I used to get fed up with making the effort. But suddenly I realized that I did love him. He was heroic and dignified as he was dying and this became greater with his return to the Church.

There had been a tremendous amount of perhaps what one would describe as hidden sorrow in my brother's life. I think the Lord said, 'Well, you've had enough now Jeremy, I'm going to take you out of this. You'd better come home to me.' Jeremy was always the quiet introvert in the family. He always suffered the most. And if that was the way the Lord wanted to purify him and bring him to a holy death, well, that was all right by me.

In that ten months I was completely changed in some respects. Not on the surface, but the interior completely changed. I realized that on the whole most things were quite unimportant. What is important are the good old-fashioned things: death, judgement, heaven and hell. What matters is that we spread the good news as best we can, whether we're priests, religious or laity, and that we evangelize and try to bring people to Christ.

Really, at the end of the day everything else doesn't matter. It completely, to use the common jargon, focused me.

I saw in my brother's death and his illness, which was absolutely horrific in the end, a real Way of the Cross; the terrible haemorrhaging he went through made him quite Christ-like. I remember his partner Andrew turned to me and said, 'I never knew it would be like this.' And I didn't know what to expect either because I was not involved with the gay community, nor with Aids work. So I also had no idea. But from about, oh I suppose two in the afternoon, he began to haemorrhage quite violently, and then from eleven until about, oh, I don't know, an hour before he died, or even half an hour, there was this really terrible haemorrhaging, you know, where the blood was just spurting out. And I remember I was absolutely fraught because my eldest brother was down in the country and so couldn't be there. I rang up Brother Michael Hargen, a fellow friar who was nearby in our friary at Peckham and said, 'Michael ... can you come? I'm not sure he's been really converted,' because Jeremy had been received back into the Church only in the last week of his life. And Michael said, 'I think it's your problem, Stephen.' He was trying to tell me that God's love and mercy was so immense that there was nothing to worry about. God simply wants one to say 'yes' to Him and then He ties up all the loose ends of our sins and infidelities. But at that time, I really was absolutely frightened. I was even beginning to look at my hands to see if I had any cuts. Jeremy's eyes were on the whole open all the time, but, of course, he was so heavily drugged he wasn't aware. At one point I said to the nurse, 'How long can this go on for?' because physically he was still very strong. And the nurse said, 'It could go on till twelve o'clock tomorrow morning,' and I thought, 'My goodness!' Every so often I just had to go out – even if he'd died, I just couldn't have done anything about it because it was too awful.

Jeremy died at dawn. He had wanted to die on a Sunday. He was born on a Sunday, but he died at four o'clock on a Monday morning, just as the first birds were beginning to sing.

I've always had a great love for the saints and perhaps treated them rather like my parents – quite badly, you know, taken them for granted. And so I have always been aware, I think, of the supernatural. As a child I was a great one for painting religious scenes. I was constantly painting pictures of the Crucifixion, the Resurrection, the Ascension and the Assumption. I loved doing the Last Judgement, which I suppose was rather odd when you think of it. I've not come across other children doing these kinds of paintings. And yet now, when I paint, it's nothing to do with the Last Judgement. I mean, gosh, I've not done a picture of the Last Judgement since I was about 17 or 18. Now it will invariably be the Holy Family or St Joseph, because ever since my ordination, which was on the Feast of St Joseph, he has made a tremendously powerful entrance into my life. With Jeremy's death, St Joseph once more made his presence felt.

I've only dreamt of two saints in my life. One was John the Baptist and the other was St Joseph. They both featured in a dream of the Last Judgement which was rather strange because it was taking place in our sitting room, rather like a Stanley Spencer painting. I had one either side of me and that's all I can remember. I've always loved John the Baptist, especially as portrayed in Richard Strauss's opera *Salome*.

It's in the context of St Joseph that I'm very well aware of the problems that men have in the Church. Women, the lay women, together with priests and religious, have the kind of Church high ground if you like. There are any number of excellent lay women in the parish. And there are ones who cause trouble as well! And the men are there being rather dreary and drippy or just doing nothing, being sidelined. I decided there was a need for something.

This coincided with my old spirituality shifting away from Thérèse of Lisieux and Francis, who are like the eternal children in God's garden playground. I realized that with Jeremy's death and my mother's simultaneous collapse into senility, I suddenly had to grow up. So I crossed the Rubicon from being a child who was always loved and pampered, not only by my family – except by my father – but also by the friars. They could not have been kinder to me, and yet they really get it from me. I'm always ticking them off and calling them to task. It's awful, really, but they take it – they're very good, and there's no reason for them to. But I suddenly knew that I'd crossed that Rubicon. I finally realized that I had, in my forties, become a man, and to some extent a father.

Recently a secular Franciscan, Henry Mellor, has put into practice what I wanted, which was an association for fathers and husbands that would help them to be good fathers and good husbands, and to promote a devotion to St Joseph and deepen their love for God the Father. So far we've had three meetings and I think my priesthood has finally been put into the correct perspective, which is odd because I never thought it would go that way. I always used to align myself with the prophets, such as Elijah and Amos, and to think that my preaching might be as fiery as theirs. But when as a priest I began to preach, I suddenly thought, 'I'm not really preaching like that; it's not very fiery.' It was coming out in quite a measured, gentle way. I mean, I can be quite fiery on occasion. I remember during the Gulf War I reduced a congregation to absolute stunned silence with my apocalyptic fervour. But then suddenly I realized that the person I was meant to try and be like – and it would never have entered my mind in a month of Sundays – was St Joseph, who is quiet and I'm not. He is always there to help in situations of crisis.

I've always been someone who encourages, because I myself was greatly encouraged by my mother and my brothers. Jeremy was wonderful at encouraging me. One of the problems in the priesthood and religious life today is that no one encourages anybody. And the reason why they're rushing off and getting married or ending up in peculiar relationships, either with women or men, is essentially because they feel unloved; they don't feel they've had that encouragement and they don't feel they've been challenged in the right way. And so the secular priest's existence is very, very lonely, whereas ours is not.

Priests need the right kind of encouragement and love from bishops, superiors and spiritual directors. My Provincial, John Condon, who has been my spiritual director for many years, has been magnificent in this regard. There was I, very badly fathered, and this man, I could honestly say, re-fathered me – this man who has the unfortunate and painful privilege of being our Provincial in these very difficult times when we're trying to work out where we're going. I think a lot of men in the Church are sort of orphans; the women are more able to cope. Suddenly I realized that it was time for me to get on and help people, and be like Joseph for them; someone who is in the background encouraging and not making a great fuss, but helping people to grow in holiness.

FAITH, HOPE AND CHASTITY

Spiritual direction is a two-way thing; people you help certainly also help you. What I've always found a bit daunting is that so often the people who come to me have the most extraordinary mystical experiences and visionary phenomena. And I think, 'Well, I don't know what to do here. I'll just trust.' I mean, you can open the textbooks, but they don't really help. I once asked a religious sister who does spiritual direction from St Bueno's, the Jesuit retreat centre in North Wales what she did when people came to her who had had visions. 'Oh, well,' she said, 'we don't encourage it.' Well, I thought, that's not the point. If they're having them, you simply have to trust the Holy Spirit. Psychology and counselling may help, but in the end it is the Holy Spirit that undergirds everything, and reveals the secrets of the soul.

An example would be the phenomena of lights. Apparently St John of the Cross said one should ignore the lights, but people see, I think, red, blue and white lights. From what I can gather, these are angels or possibly devils. It's harder to deal with the locution – when people hear voices. Then I think, 'Well, is this person mentally unbalanced?' because I'm inclined not to ignore psychological factors. I was offered counselling when I was on a course for formators. I thought if I'm going to be a novice master, perhaps I ought to have it so that I don't damage anybody. It was very helpful but it was only a small tool. But certainly one particular person had all these messages, some personally for me about conversion and how if we didn't convert, such and such would happen And I can think of another person who's had these kind of phenomena, a religious who is getting lots of messages. And I think, 'Gosh, there's an awful lot here.' But I think one has to be aware that it is essentially a private experience for that person and visionaries should not be exposed to celebrity. To understand whether these people are authentic is no easy matter. You have to test the authenticity of the person before you can assess the authenticity of the experience.

In my own life in the last six or seven years I have had two extraordinary dreams. In one I was by the shore of a lake which was surrounded by craggy cliffs and beautiful fir trees – it was a bit like a Chinese painting – I saw this naked young man dart past trying to hunt a stag or something and I realized he was

Satan. I don't know why Satan should manifest himself like that, but anyway at the next moment there was this warrior king with all his warriors around him, looking as if they'd come out of the terracotta army in China. And this tall, bearded warrior king came up and embraced me and said, 'I am God.' So it was obviously the Father and I remember saying in the dream, 'How very C. S. Lewis!'

I have always wanted to be a saint and I know it sounds like – the French put it better than the English – *folie de grandeur*, delusions of grandeur, but the more I've thought about it, the more I realize it isn't a delusion. We're all called to be saints, and when I get up and preach I tell people this because so often it was only priests and religious who were expected to be holy. Our normal calling by our baptism is to holiness – that is the normal thing as Christians. Other people don't have this, they've got to get on with whatever they can. The Holy Spirit is still working, there's no doubt about it; it is not constrained by the sacraments, but it's that bit more difficult if you are an animist, or a Hindu having to placate any number of deities. Holiness and sanctity is really not something that we do. It's what God does to us. And in my own spiritual life as a priest, as a friar, as Stephen de Kerdrel, it's been pared down to 'Thy will be done' and 'Be it done unto me according to Your word', and really nothing else matters. As a young child I always thought that things had to be *done*. I remember being very impressed by the children at Fatima and deciding to imitate one of them – Francisco – by tying a piece of knotted string round my waist as a penance. Well, I was in the school playground and after half an hour I thought, 'Oh, this is too much,' and I took it off. So I'm not able to manage any of the great penances or anything.

It is when one realizes that one has absolutely nothing to offer that one comes to God with empty hands, and He just begins to fill them. And I think to myself, 'Why are these things happening, these good things? Why?' Because God is good. It's to do with just constantly giving God one's life. Look, here it is, God. Whatever you want, have it. I mean, I do occasionally add the rider: as long as you make the shoulders broad enough to take it. And certainly in the last several years in my own life I've found this tremendous sort of joy bubbling up. I remember my guardian saying, 'I don't know how you can be so joyful with everything going on.' Well, I didn't know either. It was supernatural. It's realizing that this is a pure gift. It's to do with just being constant in our gratitude to God. If God has given Himself to us in Jesus, then we've constantly got to be giving ourselves back, whatever our vocation is. If it's marriage, we mirror the Trinity and the Holy Family. If it's religious life, we imitate Jesus. But again and again I think all these vocations dovetail, and we're in it together. So I've moved from being very individualistic and competitive as a child and wanting to be a saint, to realizing that we're all called to holiness and no one is to be left out. Obviously we're not all going to become like some of the canonized saints because that would be ridiculous, and some of the greatest saints haven't actually been canonized. But I think I see my vocation now as essentially that of a brother, a servant, a fellow traveller, and someone who is just there to encourage and say, 'Yes, you are called. We're all called to this great vocation and, you know, it's not as difficult as we think.'

I was always worried about sin as a child, whereas now I would say that it's not that one's sins don't matter but that they're not very important. What is important is this great love of God that spills over into our lives, if we only let Him, if we trust Him. And so, in my own life, I suppose my trust has become very strong. The great thing is – and this is what my brother's death and my mother's senility have taught me – you're not absolved from the pain. You've got to go through it. But you can do it, because God is with you.

I think we're coming to the end of Western civilization – of that I'm sure, I'm convinced. I don't know whether it's the end of the world, but I think that in the next 20 or so years life will be extraordinarily different. We will be living in a completely different world and it will be a world of peace. But we will have to go through a great purification. Of that I'm in no doubt. I mean, I wish I could say, 'No, I don't think Western civilization is going to be destroyed.' Sometimes I think, 'Oh, Stephen, perhaps you are too apocalyptic,' but recently I've been reading the Russian historical philosopher Berdyaev and here I see an intellectual dealing with it and saying much the same thing.

In twentieth-century Western society we turn to selfishness and sin and we make everything the object. Even Communism was a materialism. When you reduce everything to objects and rights – 'I can have a baby, it's my right' – the whole civilization weakens. It's all leisure and pleasure and nothing is gained by suffering or challenge. I think great cultural changes come about because of the few, as Berdyaev believed. It's almost an aristocratic thing – not a snobby thing. Society may not be particularly wonderful, but you have the Renaissance coming out of this time of hardship for the Church.

The mediaeval period was a great period but it wasn't high civilization like Roman civilization. Now we've reached the same kind of civilization as the Roman Empire and all we can do is just organize and manage and destroy the environment. That's all we can do; we can't actually be very creative. For all the permissiveness, there is almost no passion in society. It's either violence or a kind of jellyfish-like inertia. There doesn't seem to be anything else. So the Lord will have to bring it to a close so that we can all revive. I've always been apocalyptic by nature; in some ways that's quite Franciscan, but now it's much healthier. It's about the Lord and Jesus coming in glory. It's not so much about judgement, it's about everything being drawn to a wonderful close.

16. Father Desmond Forristal

Fr Desmond Forrestal was born in Glasnevin, Ireland in 1930

Fr Desmond Forristal, parish priest of Dalkey, a wealthy Dublin suburb, was the last priest I interviewed. I was keen to hear his views on the Irish Church in general and his own parish in particular. Moreover, I had heard of Fr Desmond's long-standing involvement in both television and theatre – he produced literally hundreds of religious documentaries as well as writing thought- provoking and successful plays. While not expecting a 'luvvie', I nevertheless looked forward to a mighty good conversationalist. This was not the case.

After a light lunch, Fr Desmond and I got down to the business of the interview. Now in his sixties, his face and even his manner reminded me slightly of Clint Eastwood: glassy eyes squinting against imaginary sunlight, sharp cheekbones and even – worryingly – the clipped speech.

My appetite had been further whetted by the fact that the late Archbishop of Dublin, Archbishop McQuaid, had forbidden Fr Desmond to write religious articles unless they were first vetted. So off-putting was this that Fr Desmond simply stopped writing for a period of 11 years – until after the Archbishop's retirement.

I realized very quickly that Fr Desmond was not prepared to look back on his experiences in the world of television and theatre in order to draw interesting and thoughtful conclusions from them. We moved on. Why, I wondered, was he effectively suspended from writing? Apparently it boiled down to style – not reverential enough. I pressed him on possible theological *differences. Nothing. For example, the issue of women priests, he said, was still unclear – the task ahead was to discern the will of the Lord. Celibacy and eucharistic sharing, he went on – these were all issues which would continue to 'come up'.*

What about feelings, the ups and downs of being a priest? 'They're not important,' he said. 'We won't be judged on our feelings, only on how much we have loved and how much we have given.' I laboured on. After much hesitation, Fr Desmond did agree to talk about the Church in Ireland and the changes it has experienced over the last few years. He was reluctant, however, to opine, preferring direct experience and even statistics to the world of ideas and intimations.

Fr Desmond's reserve left me perplexed. Either he was hiding important information – be it concrete facts or his own personal views – or he was simply demonstrating the humility that comes from years of prayer and personal reflection. I am still not sure – but at the risk of being a fool, the answer, I feel, is probably the latter.

The Church in Ireland is not as organized as the English Church. There's always an element of luck in anything that happens in Ireland – coming to Mass on time, for example, or coming to anything on time, for that matter, is not in the Irish nature. There's a kind of irresponsibility, a certain vagueness ... I don't know, I don't want to make a caricature of the Irish, but there's always that element in Irish religion. I think that one of the great dangers for Irish people at the moment – and I am sure they're just picking it up from abroad – is the rejection of commitment, particularly lifelong commitment. The priesthood as a lifelong commitment has obviously been rejected by those who either don't want to become priests, or become priests but decide after three or four years that they want out.

It's very much the same with marriage. There's been a rise in the number of people who just don't get married but have relationships or partners or whatever word you want to use. They're not prepared to commit themselves to another person, to a family, to children. And of course marriages break up, and again loyalty to the wife and the children is just thrown away. Now that's a threat to the very foundations of society and I think the English don't realize the trouble that's lying in store for them in the very near future, due to the number of children growing up without a father, without any authority, without any images to imitate and without any knowledge of what it is to live in a family. This is something horrific. I don't think it has ever happened in history before, but it's happening not only in England but throughout the world and it's beginning to come to Ireland as well.

It reminds me of an alcoholic. They say an alcoholic will never try to cure himself until he hits the bottom. He's actually got to go down until he can't go any further and then he begins to rise again. I think this could happen in Western civilization. We'll reach the point of such social disaster that there'll be no way to go except to turn the other way and bring back all these commitments and loyalties and ways of living life. That's the only way. It's going to happen.

It's hard for me to know when I got the idea of a vocation because it seems to have been an idea that was always there. I don't remember actually making a decision at any stage, although certainly as a youngster of six or seven I had it in mind to be a priest. I didn't think about it that much but I do remember saying Mass, as it were, in the bathroom with my little brother as the altar boy. I was robed in a big bath towel and he had to kneel behind me and ring the bell whenever I told him to.

My mother's brother, my uncle, was a priest, though I didn't know him. He went out to South Africa as a missionary and then World War Two intervened, after which there was a period of about ten years when nobody could travel from South Africa to Ireland. But he was there, certainly, in the background.

My father died from a brain tumour at the age of 43, leaving my mother to go back to her work in the Civil Service and keep the house going for her two sons. We ended up in Belvedere College, a very well-known and reputable Jesuit school where James Joyce studied as a youngster. I thought about the Jesuits for a while and was quite interested, but I was sent by one of them to a spiritual director and I think he over-estimated my sanctity. He said I would have to empty my mind of thoughts of anything except God; I mustn't think about anything because it would divert me from Him. I thought this was a bit much so I said,

'Could I not even have a piece of music in my mind?' – because I love singing things in my mind. 'No,' he said, 'No, that wouldn't do!' I obviously wasn't up to his standard, so I walked home and never went back again.

Seminary days were very happy, I must say; I got on very well – lots of good company. There were 22 of us who started at Clonliffe College on the same day and we got to know each other very well. I drifted into the priesthood because nothing ever occurred to me that would change my mind. There was no flash of light, no voices in the night or anything like that, no visions, nothing dramatic or picturesque. It was just ... if you believe in God, if you believe in the Eucharist, if you believe in the people of God, it seemed obvious that the most fulfilling possible vocation was to be a priest and to serve the people of God and be their minister. That seemed the best thing to do.

Once or twice I've found myself in a parish with another priest who I didn't get on with and those have been the hardest times. I've always found that if you get on well with the priests, you'll be happy in that parish, no matter where it is, and likewise if you're not happy with the priests, you won't. Even though everybody else is nice, you won't be happy because in the priesthood there's a brotherhood, and if you feel betrayed or not supported by your brothers then it's very sad and very demoralizing.

Celibacy hasn't been particularly hard because we were prepared for it in the seminary; we were taught how to live alone. We each had our own room where we studied for up to two hours before coming down to meet others. There was a sense that you had to be able to survive on your own, you mustn't need the support of people all the time. Perhaps the modern seminary, which is much more informal, is not altogether doing a service to priests because they will find it even more difficult to live alone if they're used to company all the time. I wanted the whole package and that included the celibacy. Of course there have been times when I've felt lonely and times when I've come in at night and had to open the door on to a dark and cold house. On the other hand, there have been times when I've been exhausted and I've gone home and it's been great to sit down and kick off my shoes and not have to talk to anybody.

I used to write the odd piece for *The Furrow*, a very reputable Catholic magazine at the time. I remember writing about the centenary of Clonliffe College. It was an ordinary kind of piece, but I always feel that when you're writing you have to make it readable or people will leave you after line three. Certainly I do that when reading somebody else. So I adopted a reasonably cheerful, lighthearted tone but this didn't meet with Archbishop McQuaid's approval. I made comments about the central heating system which weren't altogether complimentary and also about the background of Cardinal Cullen, who founded the seminary and who was extremely Roman in his outlook. I described Clonliffe College as a bastion of Rome on the banks of the Tolka – that's a small stream that meandered through the grounds of the seminary – it certainly wasn't the Tiber. But he was outraged at this sort of thing. I did one or two others that seemed to be quite innocent and enjoyable but he then issued a sort of fatwa. He didn't actually suspend me, but he laid down rules that I had to bring anything I wrote to a priest whom he named and have it approved by him before it could be published. This was so burdensome that I just stopped, at least for a long period. I managed to keep my head anyhow.

At that stage nothing terribly controversial had come up in terms of theology. It was during Vatican II all right, but before Archbishop John Charles had decided that Vatican II was a Bad Thing, which he later did. So I can't identify any theological difference. I think it was more the fact that I didn't have a reverential style, which is all that matters. I remember his pastoral letters, which had to be read out by the clergy and which were a great penance both for us and for the laity because they sounded as though they'd been translated from the Latin. Maybe he felt annoyed that he couldn't communicate in the way that other people could, I don't know.

With respect to women priests I would say the problem is not should they be allowed, but have they been allowed – does God allow them? If He does allow them, then we can go and ordain women and they'll be priests. If He doesn't, we can ordain them and they won't be priests. This may sound a bit abstruse, but we don't know what the Lord's will is. For instance, we have here in Ireland a so-called bishop – illegally ordained – who himself ordained a woman priest recently. But is she a priest? For example, if she says in the Mass, 'This is my body', well, is it? Is it a

Mass? Or is it just somebody pretending? How do we know? We only know by the Holy Spirit speaking through the Church, and certainly the Holy Spirit has in the past made it clear through the teaching of the Church that it is men who are ordained as priests. The answer is I don't know but I believe it will become clear.

There have been a whole lot of changes in the Church here in Ireland recently. There used to be a tremendous reverence for the Church and for priests and perhaps that wasn't very good for a young man. It would go to his head a bit, the feeling that he was a source of all sorts of wisdom and holiness and everybody respected him and even revered him. That passed away, rather quickly and rather suddenly. It started with the trial of the paedophile priest – Father Brendan Smyth – and then another wad of cases came up. It was a great shock, and not only to lay people but to other priests who didn't know that this was going on and were absolutely horrified. It has caused a demoralization among priests and has had a big effect on young men who are thinking of the priesthood; a lot of the appeal of priesthood has gone, combined with the fact that the law of celibacy is increasingly attacked and undermined by those who are opposed to it.

The practice of religion has also gone off target as a result of this. The complaint I hear all the time is that Mass is boring. I suppose if you want to be bored, you'll be bored since it's certainly not entertainment. It also depends on what you mean by boring. If you were to put me into a nightclub with all the lights out and all the music like thunder rattling in my ears, I wouldn't just find it boring, I'd regard it as extreme persecution, but that doesn't mean that other people don't enjoy it and get a lot out of it. But it's not just things like Mass being boring. There's also a rapidly growing materialism. There's always been a very strong element of the spiritual in Ireland and a closeness to God and to angels and maybe even to things like fairies and leprechauns and such like. But that sort of spirituality is going. A friend of mine, a priest, said the coming of the electric light in Ireland put an end to ghost stories, which is probably true, because ghosts thrive where there are oil lamps flickering, not when you switch on a 40-watt bulb. But it's money now and materialism that are becoming more and more important. Young people are choosing walks of life in which they dedicate themselves to how much they'll be paid and what they can afford. This is becoming more and more central to the Irish mind. A lot of the quaintness seems to have gone.

There are certainly a lot of wealthy people here in Dalkey, and poorer people too, though not so many. I find the poorer people are far more religious on the whole than the richer people – financially the parish is supported by the poor, not by the rich. A lot of these people have become millionaires because they don't give money away; that's what they have chosen and that's the way they live. I don't actually know how many people in the Church are wealthy, but you can guess by their dress and where they live and so on. There has always been that sort of tension in Christianity between God and Mammon; we've had to serve them both at the same time. But if you choose money wholeheartedly then you've chosen against God. It's very hard for rich people to come near to God if riches have become the mainstream of their lives. One can be wealthy as well as a good Christian by living life in accordance with the commandments, by being honest and upright, by being generous with what you have and by remembering what is most important in life. But you have to use your riches very thoughtfully.

People say the Church should move with the times but that's not for the Church. The Church is here to move the times, not to follow them. You know the story of the politician who ends his speech with, 'Those are my principles, and if you don't like them I'll change them.' That's what we're fighting against. Maybe you can end up entrenched in certain attitudes, but it's better to be entrenched than to lie. There must be some principles and some certainties. People don't want uncertainties now; they have their own uncertainties – they don't want any more.

I think one thing that's very important for the Irish, or certainly has been in the past, is their love for the Church. The Irish Church has a different relationship with its people compared to virtually any other country because for almost as long as we can remember the Irish Church has been the underdog. Persecuted by the prevailing authorities, namely of course the English authorities, it has shared the suffering of the people. It has never been an establishment church, never a comfortable church, never a church that's been given privileges. It has been a hunted church and a harried church and so often a church of sadness rather than a church of joy. Inevitably when that stops it changes attitudes, because after the Free State the Church became virtually an established church – a revered church for whom nothing was too good. Everything was done in accordance with the Church and that was part of the reason why the Irish started to drift away. The old feeling that the priest was sharing their suffering and their hardships and their poverty and even their imprisonment and their executions was something that was a tremendous blood force that united the Irish people to their Church.

Something rather similar has happened in Eastern Europe. In Poland, for example, the Church was much stronger under Polish Communist persecution than it is now that Communism has gone. If the Church has everything its own way, if the Church becomes part of the establishment, it's not a good thing, because the Lord himself said, 'If they persecuted me, they will persecute you.' And if nobody's persecuting us somewhere, sometime, about something, then maybe we're not doing our job.

17. Brother Benedict Kiely OFMCap

Br Benedict Kiely was born in London in 1963

At the age of 36 Brother Ben is the youngest Franciscan priest in Britain. He was attracted to a religious Order mainly because of the companionship such a way of life offers; the prospect of a presbytery, and the loneliness that can entail, was not for him. At the age of 18, having recognized his vocation he opted for the Capuchin Franciscans – renowned for their strict rules of poverty and simplicity. But after four years of study and preparation, Brother Ben decided that he was not ready to commit himself to the final three and so embarked upon a life outside the Order. It is at this point that we pick up the story – a story which recounts, often humorously, one hurdle after another on the path to final vows and which ends with a love affair and a crisis of conscience that was to change Brother Ben for ever.

I left the Franciscan Order in 1986 after an initial four years of training and didn't know what the heck I was going to do. At the age of 22 I hadn't even written a cheque before. I thought I might come back to the Order one day, if I didn't get married instead, but if it was meant to be it would happen in God's good time. I had been a rather dogmatic 18-year-old when I approached the Order and I think I was lucky that they actually let me join at that age. I didn't regret joining young because I knew it had given me a good grounding, but I also knew I needed some experience of life.

The idea of a 'call' conjures up Cecil B. De Mille films with Charlton Heston and voices coming from behind curtains. Some people must get that but not many. For me it tended to be feelings that I fitted into something, that it felt right. The feeling of wanting to be a priest seemed to come from nowhere, so that might have been a call. It came out of nowhere and it also became more mature. If you get through the whole seven-year process of temporary vows and you decide to make that commitment, perhaps then it is clearer that there is a call. In the Church's eyes, that's the proof that you are called even if many subsequently leave. In the eyes of the Church once you are accepted, your call is valid.

Once outside the Order I went from the sublime to the ridiculous. Within two and a half months of leaving I was working in a very small PR company, through a friend who had got me in at the bottom to do basic jobs like stamp-licking, but then also writing press releases. I had a very good boss who taught me well and is now an extremely successful marketing person in America. So I did PR for computer games in the mid-1980s when computer games were really booming, all of which I found quite horrendous. I didn't enjoy the selling part of public relations. I never enjoyed selling anything, not even God! But I enjoyed the creative side and you have to be pretty creative when you're trying to sell computer games.

After a year I got a job in Foyle's, the bookshop. The unique distinction of Foyle's is that if you are qualified in any particular area, they immediately put you in the department for which you are not qualified. So foolish me, thinking that maybe I would be put in Theology, was put straight into Travel and then into the Receiving Department, which is where all the lorries come in to unload. I ended up managing that department, which brought in all the books for the shop. It was basically very hard physical work unloading 40-kilo boxes every day off lorries, but it was interesting in its own unique way. Obviously it wasn't intellectually stimulating, but Foyle's was excellent for the people who were there. Foyle's, with its antiquated payment system, was quite a Dickensian sort of place. However, there was a vaguely 'university' atmosphere. 'Miss' Foyle, a twentieth-century Miss Haversham, employed only graduates or unusual people and I was on their list I suppose, as one of the unusual people. When new staff began, they would be taken all over the store and, as the icing on the cake of the store's weirdness, they would be told, 'There's even an ex-monk in Receiving!'

After a year I decided to leave and go to Australia because I was 26 and I knew that I could get a work permit. I thought this would be a supreme adventure because I didn't know anybody at all out there. So I didn't tell anyone; I just got it all arranged and then at the last minute told my parents where I was going. Again I didn't know what the heck was going to happen but it was very far away and I just wanted to do it.

It rained constantly in Sydney which I hadn't expected at all. The rain was really unbelievable – non-stop, 24-hour, heavy tropical rain. For the first three months I worked all week and it rained all weekend. I had never experienced how depressing weather could be; it was utterly depressing to have every single weekend washed out. But then the weather started to improve and I met a young lady who came to work in the shop. I was 26 years old and she was my first girlfriend. I had been in a single-sex boarding school from the age of eight, after which I went straight into the Order at the age of 18, so there hadn't been that much 'dating' as they say; you certainly weren't encouraged to do it in the Order. I thought we would just be friends and that would be that but then she kind of made the move on me, which was quite an unusual experience. We used to go and have a drink regularly after work. She was finishing with her boyfriend, and one day she told me that she really liked me and wanted a relationship with me and didn't want to be 'just friends'! So, yes, at the age of 26 I moved from 'virgo intacta' (if a man can be!) to non-virgin status. Strangely enough I had no moral dilemma about it – my religious practice was not exactly fanatical at the time. We were extreme opposites. She was quite anti-Catholic – in fact she was the great, great grand-niece of Australia's first and recently beatified Mother Mary McKillop. But she was nothing like Mother Mary McKillop, that's for sure.

She wasn't a communicative person. She was quite closed-in about feelings and things like that and so she never said she loved me or anything. I can't remember if I ever said I loved her but, on the day I left, she told me she loved me at the airport, which I thought was, you know, typical of a woman. I know that sounds a bit sexist, but we're allowed a bit of that aren't we?

I mean it was a bit late to be telling me she loved me just as I was about to fly to a country 15,000 miles away.

It's peculiar looking back on it. I did more of the work in terms of communication, but then she sort of flipped round at the end and I suppose she enjoyed the fact that I did communicate with her, maybe more than an Australian male would. The crucial point is that it was in Australia that I began to think about coming back to the Order. I thought, 'Well, what am I going to do with the rest of my life?' and it just began to feel right that I should come back. But I didn't want to come back immediately so I decided to return to England and do one more job, just for the experience. I became a bus driver – much to my parents' horror after they had spent so much money on my education. I went to the Shepherd's Bush garage in London and passed my double-decker bus driving test and drove a double-decker bus for three months. It was a horrendous experience driving through all the worst parts of London traffic – Piccadilly Circus, Trafalgar Square and so on. Three months was all I could manage.

I returned to the Order in 1990 having been out for four years – I was in for four years and out for four years. I took my 'simple vows' as they're called, which last for three years, and then in 1992 I went to America as part of my final training. The Franciscan Order worldwide is divided into provinces and I went to the province of mid-America, which is basically Colorado, Missouri and Kansas. The idea is that during the year before final vows one has an experience of life in another province of the Order – a different kind of ministry and a different kind of culture. I went to a parish in Colorado which was 98 per cent black. I also did one day a week at a very well-run homeless shelter owned by the Friars. It was a multi-million dollar, purpose-built shelter with a paid staff of about 30; psychologists, counsellors – the lot. I was nervous about working there initially. Many of the homeless are mentally ill and they used to have an armed police officer on duty in the shelter. On one occasion the officer had to draw his gun on one of the residents who was holding a knife. But I really enjoyed my time there. I think it was because of the very proactive way the staff tried to break the cycle of homelessness with the training, counselling and the residential programmes. Instead of just complaining about homelessness, I was involved in something real and positive.

The American friars are much freer than us. In the evenings we'd eat out or see a film or a baseball match or something like that. They have a different view of the Franciscan notion of 'recreation', you see. We do it a bit here but we are much more formal. Perhaps the English side has a bit more structure, certainly in terms of prayer and things like that. In America we only really met for prayer in the mornings because they were all so busy. They all went out from the friary to different jobs and maybe only a couple would meet at the end of the day for evening prayer. That would never happen in England; we always have those regular gatherings.

Anyway I was in this black parish and that was an excellent experience. It had a full gospel choir and I was fully involved in all sorts of ministry, working with community organizations and in particular with the police who were dealing with the gang problems they have there. Kids join these gangs and I don't mean gangs like 'Just William'; they have machine guns and it's serious. So there's a police unit dedicated to the gang problem. They have hundreds and thousands of kids' names on computer and they identify them as they are driving along by the colours they wear. There was a gang problem just around our church, which is why I had the link with them. It's frightening when they've got their guns out because suddenly it's not the movies; the guns are real and you know that at any moment there could be shooting. But it was also quite exciting. Obviously I didn't want people to be shot for my entertainment but it was exciting. It was also good to see the Church really involved with the local community.

In the American Church, with all its faults and failings, people are there because they want to go to church. Their whole idea of Mass obligation is long gone. I mean people go because they want to, not because they are told to, and they want to be fully committed to the life of the Church. The Americans are incredibly busy. Many people I met had two jobs, some even had three. So they have virtually no spare time but what they have, they give to the Church even though they have families.

I'd never really mixed with black people, which sounds unusual but I'd certainly never been the only white person in a room before. That took a bit of getting used to but it was a tremendous experience just to talk to people. One of them told me he could never be friends with a white American because of his experience of racism. All his white friends, he said, were foreign; it was another experience of growing. I was also preaching, which was an excellent training because they were very responsive – unlike British congregations where a stifled yawn is often the most dynamic reaction to a sermon. In America they responded to you and they expected a good homily.

I was happy in America and I was almost at the end of my training, which is why what I'm about to reveal was so unusual. I was planning to return in September and everything was going fine and dandy, as they say. In July I'd met a friend of a friend called Judy, who worked in the shelter as a probation officer. We chatted and it turned out our birthdays were within two days of each other, and so we decided to go out with other people on a kind of joint birthday thing. We did that and we became friendly and then we met up again a few times. I began to realize that this was what the Americans call 'dating behaviour' which was not appropriate for me but I thought, 'Well, what the heck, nothing's going to happen and anyway I'll be back in a couple of weeks,' because this was well into August now. We then went out to dinner and for some bizarre reason she said, 'Let's go to New Mexico this evening.' I thought this would be a grand choice but in fact we couldn't go until the next day. It was seven hours' drive to New Mexico but Americans do that sort of thing. I always wanted to be in a road movie – you know, these movies where people go off through places like New Mexico and have weird adventures. Anyway, we went to New Mexico and to cut an extremely long story short we became involved – which I hadn't expected and hadn't intended. You know the scenes in the old Hollywood movies – the hotel door closes, the waves crash on the shore, the train goes into the tunnel ... I'm not saying I was naïve because I wasn't, but all the way up to the point of departure, euphemistically speaking, I really didn't intend anything to happen. But it happened anyway and then everything became compressed into the next few weeks.

Looking back on it now, it was a holiday romance really – a holiday romance which shouldn't have happened. It was then blown up out of proportion because of the artificial situation I was in. We couldn't meet in public; we couldn't just get to know

FAITH, HOPE AND CHASTITY

each other and wander round a city as any other young man and woman would. It wasn't furtive – we weren't scurrying around – but for two weeks it was intense, and so, for some bizarre reason, we decided to get married. If we had got to know each other properly we would have realized we were not compatible and it would have just been normal like anybody else. But I was still very 'black and white' about life. Even though I knew it was not really what I wanted, I thought, 'Well, I've become involved with somebody, so I must leave the Order.' It was like a railway train heading towards marriage and it horrified me. Basically I was riddled with guilt. Even though I was not yet ordained as a priest, I had broken the rules and, with the Church's demonizing of sex, had broken them big-time. I had yet to discover that we all make mistakes and that to forgive ourselves is often the hardest thing to do.

Obviously there were all the normal, external chemical feelings – all the nice stuff – but then there were lots of intimations as well which I didn't pay much attention to. It was so short, you see, and the principal thing pushing me was this sense of right and wrong. Once I was back in England she planned a trip to London and I just knew I couldn't be in the friary and see her at the same time. I was very much against the idea of living any kind of a lie so I had to make a clear-cut decision. I came back and told my superior I wanted to leave. In fact he put me on a leave of absence, which was a great saving.

Anyway, she came over for a week and we had a big row, because she wanted to go and look at wedding dresses and I just didn't want to. It was becoming patently obvious that this was not meant to be because I really wasn't happy – I wanted to be in the Order. Maybe if I had really been in love with her – and this is the thing I'll never know – it would have been completely different, but I didn't want this to happen and so it was a very unpleasant experience. The other problem was that in order to go back to America I would have had to marry her, because I couldn't get a job without being married to an American citizen and this was yet another pressure. It was a real rollercoaster thing.

Anyway, we got to November and I went out to see her for a fortnight. It was then that I knew I had made the greatest mistake. We were both miserable and we had to end it. I obviously felt really bad about any pain I caused but she was not naïve. We both made a big mistake and I had nearly destroyed my future, and if we had continued we would have ended up as very unhappy people. I came back, explained everything to my boss and then had to eat excessive helpings of humble pie, which wasn't enjoyable. The whole experience was not enjoyable. This sort of thing happens to lots of people without becoming public, but because of my ultra 'right and wrong' approach I thought I had to leave the Order. I had made it public when most people would have had the experience, luxuriated in a good dose of Catholic guilt and then come back home and got on with life. I felt that I had to do right by God, the Order and Judy – a combination which really didn't add up. It was all so public. I made a fool of myself.

In retrospect, it taught me that there are more grey areas in life than black and white ones; there's nothing wrong with being a human being. It also taught me to be more forgiving. This sounds like an awful American self-help book: 'I'm OK, You're OK'. Well, 'I'm Reasonably All Right' would be my book! I had to be a bit more forgiving of myself; I needed to know that I could make a mistake. It could have gone the other way and made me much worse – a sort of extreme Plymouth Brethren type.

I don't think it's necessary for a priest to be celibate. There are all sorts of utilitarian arguments about why priests should be celibate but I think one can be a perfectly good priest without being celibate. Celibacy is a gift and a call but it is not necessarily the same as the call to the priesthood. If the law were to change tomorrow, secular priests who live and work in parishes could marry. As friars we couldn't because we have taken a vow of chastity. So even if the Pope decided that from now on priests could marry, I would not be able to. You might, however, get hundreds of monks transferring to dioceses so that they could become secular priests and a lot, I mean a lot, admit that they became religious priests or brothers mainly for the company. But yes, the non-politician's answer is that it is a law which is unfairly imposed. There is no actual choice. If you want to be a priest, and feel called to be a priest, you must be celibate. There is no free choice in that.

Rabbis are married and God blesses the family. In Genesis it says, 'It is not good for man to be alone' and, 'Go forth and

FAITH, HOPE AND CHASTITY

multiply'. So we have to find God in the real world, that's what the incarnation is all about. The old theology expounded chastity, poverty and obedience as the more perfect state; you were meant to be living the Kingdom of God's values on earth. That's all well and good but today a religious vocation is seen more as a way of living your baptism. It's *a* way, not *the* way. It's not a better way and for some who are called to the religious life – there's no doubt about it – they can be closer to God, because that's the way they are called. But if you are called to married life, which the vast majority of Christians are, then you can find God as well – but you have to find God in the nitty-gritty and hurly-burly of married life. It's probably more difficult to be a married person and a Christian and also to live and work in 'the world' than it is to be a priest.

It is also difficult being a priest in a very secular country like Britain. One of the friars went out recently to buy a new telephone. He was still in his habit and it was home-time at the local school, so of course he provided tremendous entertainment for the kids. They were shouting 'Friar Tuck' and things like that; that's the only connection they have with a friar. They have no concept really of what this means, of why this fellow is wearing this weird outfit. It's something from the history books. For those children the idea that there could be people like that today is bizarre, whereas in a Catholic country like Italy, the sight of friars, monks, nuns or whatever walking around is quite normal. Even though the people might not be practising, the culture supports it. In a very secular state indifference is one of the hardest things to deal with.

There's also this whole business of Mass attendance dropping off. It's not that people are anti, it's just that they don't care – they're drifting away. There's a kind of treacly spirituality around whereby people pop into church once in a blue moon and then pop out again. Even over the last ten years a lot of the support has gone with the reporting of so many scandals. Respect for the priest has gone, which is perhaps a good thing because it did tend to let priests get away with murder, but there really isn't much respect for the priesthood – even within the Catholic community. I think that makes it much more difficult to be a priest because you don't have those external props. Maybe we are getting back to a purer Church in one way. Maybe through all of this we will eventually be a much purer Church because it will be more like the original Church, which didn't have those supports.

Catholics are more accepted in society but we are also more like everybody else now. We used to be more like the Jews with our special practices, our days in the week when we went to church and our funny traditions like not eating meat on Fridays. There were all sorts of cultural things that made us a bit different as Catholics. That's all pretty much gone now. We're so assimilated into society that in a sense the idea of a counter-culture isn't there any more. And yet as friars that's exactly what we should be encouraging. Certainly that's what we are meant to do. We're meant to be saying that materialism is not the be-all and end-all and that a simple life is better.

The ideal of religious life is wonderful; it's a marvellous inspiration. For 800 years people have followed St Francis because of his closeness to Christ. He was called another Christ very early on by his brothers and by all the people around him. He is probably the most famous saint in the world and is loved and revered by Hindus and Moslems as well. There's also the image of him surrounded by birds; he was a sort of mediaeval Doctor Doolittle. There's a tremendous inspiration in the idea of fraternity, of joining a brotherhood where we are a true communistic society, living a life of simplicity, giving in all our earnings and drawing from the common pot. The difference between the ideal and the reality is, of course, strong. In the priesthood we are human beings and there is always a danger of cynicism which is corrosive. That has to be guarded against and there is a constant stream in theology which is always renewing our thinking and trying to go back to the original inspiration.

The Order in this country is very top-heavy with older men. There are only three of us under 40 in final vows and so the prospects, humanly speaking, are not wonderful. However, St Francis started it with only one other brother and when the friars arrived in England in 1223 there were only nine of them. Within 100 years there were a thousand, so numbers don't really matter.

I don't regret anything actually, to be honest with you. It doesn't mean that I don't regret sin, but even Julian of Norwich said that sin in the end can be used by God to teach you lessons and bring you closer to God. I certainly don't regret the confusion of some aspects of my life; I think life is more confused than clear most of the time. I believe St Irenaeus when he said, 'The glory of God is a human being fully alive.' I think it's the task of everybody to know what it means to be fully alive. I also have a personal motto, which is from 'The Song of the Open Road' by the American Walt Whitman: 'Whoever you are come follow me. Travelling with me you find what never tires.' I am on a sort of journey and I don't really know where it's going. But I do believe that if one tries to be faithful, then ultimately God will look after you. I'm not that worried. I believe God will see me right in the end.